SELMA EVANS

CO-PARENTING WITH A NARCISSIST

BREAK FREE FROM THE CYCLE OF EMOTIONAL ABUSE AND PROTECT YOUR CHILDREN'S WELL-BEING

TABLE OF CONTENTS

INTRODUCTION

Long before someone took the first selfie, there was a fable in ancient Greek and Roman mythology about a man who was a little too preoccupied with his image. According to one version of events, Narcissus was a lovely young man roaming the world in quest of a woman to adore. Having turned down the love of a nymph named Echo, he saw his reflection in the water and fell head over heels in love with it. Unfortunately, Narcissus perished because he could not bear to be separated from his beloved. The Narcissus flower grew near where he died, so we named it after it.

Essentially, the myth depicts narcissism as excessive self-involvement, even to the harm of others. However, narcissism is a collection of characteristics that have been investigated and classified by psychologists. Narcissism is characterized by an exaggerated sense of one's importance. Narcissists, in varying degrees, believe they are superior to others in terms of appearance, intelligence, and importance, and that they are deserving of special attention.

Psychologists distinguish between grandiose and vulnerable narcissism when describing narcissism as a personality feature. We will come back to narcissistic personality disorder, which is a more severe variety, in a moment. However, a common type of grandiose narcissism involves excessive extroversion, dominance, and the desire for attention. Grandiose narcissists are often found in positions of authority, such as politics, the media, or the arts.

People who seek power and positions of authority are not all egotistical, of course. For many, the motivation is noble: realizing their full potential or improving the lives of many others. But, at the same time, narcissistic people aim for power because of the attention and status it brings.

Those who are weak and vulnerable to narcissism tend to be reserved. However, they are vulnerable to being intimidated or slighted because of their strong sense of entitlement. In either case, narcissism has a negative side that manifests itself over time.

Because narcissists are self-centered, they may make risky or unethical actions or be disloyal in relationships. Resentment and aggression might set in when their sunny self-perception is challenged. It is like having an illness that makes you feel great, but affects everyone around you.

Narcissistic personality disorder is a medical term for this type of behavior taken to its logical conclusion.

One to two percent of the population is affected, with men being the most frequently affected. It is a diagnosis that is only given to adults. It is pretty normal for children and teenagers to be self-centered, but this is merely a growth phase. After adolescence, however, narcissism is considered a disease, according to Sigmund Freud.

The Diagnostic and Statistical Manual of Mental Disorders, 5th edition, by the American Psychiatric Association, defines various characteristics of narcissistic personality disorder. They include an inflated self-image, difficulty empathizing, a sense of entitlement, and a desire for admiration or attention. They are all symptoms of a personality disorder.

These characteristics take control of people's lives and cause substantial issues, which makes them actual personality disorders. Consider what would happen if you treated your partner or children as a means of attracting attention or appreciation instead of simply showing them care. Try telling everyone who tried to help you that they were wrong instead of asking for input on your performance to see how it would change things.

What contributes to someone becoming narcissistic?

Although we still do not know which genes are at play, we do know there is a strong genetic component. However, a person's surroundings should not be overlooked. A child's grandiose narcissism can be fostered by parents who put their child on a pedestal. Cold, strict parents might also leave their children open to narcissism. Individualism and self-promotion are highly valued in cultures where narcissism is more prevalent. Because of the rise in self-esteem and consumerism in the 1970s, narcissism has become an increasingly common personality trait in the United States. Recent developments in social media have increased the number of opportunities for self-promotion. However, there is no conclusive evidence to suggest that social media use leads to an increase in narcissism. It is just another way for egotistical individuals like narcissists to feel important. So, are there ways for narcissists to overcome their flaws?

Practicing compassion or engaging in psychotherapy, for example, can encourage self-reflection and help people care about others. The problem is that people with narcissistic personality disorder may find it difficult to continue working for self-improvement. When viewed from an unfavorable perspective, self-reflection is difficult for narcissists.

PART 1 - DYNAMICS OF NARCISSISTIC RELATIONSHIPS

CHAPTER 1: HISTORY AND NATURE OF NARCISSISM

Narcissism was diagnosed as a mental illness in 1898 by author and physician Havelock Ellis. It is known that narcissists have an exaggerated sense of self and are addicted to fantasies. However, they also have an exceptional level of calm and serenity, which is only shattered when the narcissist's self-confidence is threatened, and they tend to take people for granted or use them.

It is possible to diagnose somebody with a narcissistic personality disorder by conducting a clinical assessment. Corresponding to the *Diagnostic and Statistical Manual of Mental Disorders* (DSM-5th ed., 2013), grandiosity and attention-seeking are personality traits associated with it, as are significant impairments in personality functioning, such as looking to others for self-esteem regulation, seeing oneself as exceptional, lacking empathy, and forming superficial relationships with others.

These characteristics do not change much over time or depend on a person's developmental stage, medical condition, or usage of medicines. Narcissistic personality type is a phrase used to describe a less severe version of narcissism. Thus, a narcissistic personality disorder may be present, yet these people are within the normal range of personality traits.

A narcissistic personality disorder or the narcissistic personality type is characterized by an obsession with upholding unrealistically high expectations of oneself. Narcissists obsess about receiving affirmation that others value them, and whether they achieve or fail in doing so, they experience either tremendous joy or negative feelings. In order to get admiration, narcissists aggressively manipulate others. It is therefore considered that chronic interpersonal self-esteem regulation might manifest itself in the form of narcissism.

The Narcissistic Personality Inventory (NPI), the most extensively used scale of its kind, may be used to diagnose narcissistic personality disorder and the narcissistic personality type. The NPI asks respondents to choose between two statements that best describe them in a series of forced-choice tasks. For example, participants in the NPI will be asked if "people always appear to acknowledge my authority" or "being an authority does not mean all that much to me" best describes their personality. People with high NPI scores exhibit arrogance, pretended superiority, and violence, among other traits associated with narcissism. Narcissistic personality disorder patients perform better on the NPI than individuals with other diagnoses or in control groups because they have higher NPI scores.

Researchers believe childhood trauma might contribute to adult narcissism. This theory is endorsed by the work of Austrian psychoanalysts Heinz Kohut and Otto Kernberg. Adult narcissistic personality disorder has its roots in early social (parental) connections, according to Kohut and Kernberg. Also, both see narcissism as a flaw in the process of becoming one's true self. According to Kohut, a child's self-development and maturity are attributed to interactions with others (mainly the mother) that allow the youngster to acquire acceptance and enhancement and connect with ideal and omnipotent role models. Parents who empathize with their children help the child's self-development in two ways. First, because they reflect our true selves, they help us develop a more realistic view of ourselves. Second, parents help children absorb or assume an idealistic picture of what it takes to succeed by revealing their limits. Problems arise when parents lack empathy and fail to provide encouragement and positive role models for their children.

A child's mental growth is stopped because of narcissism, according to Kohut, and this leads to a child's self-perception that is grandiose and unrealistic. At the same time, the youngster keeps idealizing others to maintain his or her self-esteem. Narcissism, according to Kernberg's idea, is a kind of self-defense.

When a youngster reacts to their parents' coldness and lack of empathy, it might be a sign of narcissism in the parents themselves. Kernberg claims that when parents ignore their children, they grow emotionally starved and explode with wrath. Likewise, a child's attempt to seek solace in some feature of his or her personality that elicits praise from others might be seen as a narcissistic defense that ultimately leads to an exaggerated image of one's importance. Kernberg believes that narcissists may appear grandiose on the surface, but they are fragile and doubt their value on the inside.

Kernberg and Kohut argue that persons who have a history of poor social interactions as children are more likely to grow up with narcissistic ideas and become psychologically dependent on others as adults.

Findings from studies utilizing the NPI paint a picture of narcissists as having inflated and conceited views of themselves. So it is no surprise that narcissists have a high opinion of themselves. However, positive self-perceptions tend to be founded on exaggerated assessments of their achievements and misguided ideas about what other people think of them. Compared to objective measures of a person's beauty and intelligence, they exaggerate their physical attractiveness and intellectual ability. NPI findings were used to identify narcissistic and non-narcissistic males, who were then questioned by a woman, ensuring that all the men received the same social feedback. In contrast to the non-narcissistic men, narcissistic men placed a higher value on the woman's attractiveness than the former. It has also been found that narcissists are more likely to give themselves credit for favorable results, even if they happened accidentally.

Although narcissists have a high sense of self-worth, it can be shaky and unstable, as shown by their mood swings. It varies more from day to day and from moment to moment than in less narcissistic persons. Studies show that those with high explicit (self-reported) self-esteem are more likely to be narcissistic than those with high implicit (or automatic) self-esteem. Although narcissists describe themselves in a good light, this research shows that their unconscious feelings about themselves are less so. With their too optimistic and very insecure self-perceptions, narcissists are more receptive to input from others.

On the other hand, narcissists are not satisfied with merely getting any response or input from others; they want to know that other people admire and respect them. As a result, narcissists place a higher emphasis on attention and praise than on being liked and accepted. According to research, narcissists' self-esteem is influenced by how much they value being praised.

Narcissists also try to influence the impressions they leave on people to gain praise from others. Self-promotional and egotistical words are made in an attempt to gain respect and admiration from others. When they feel threatened, they lash out in rage and contempt. An angry response might harm a connection since they are more prone to behave aggressively and derogate individuals who threaten them. Narcissists want admiration from people around them, and when others fail to reciprocate, they become hostile, which exacerbates the disorder's characteristic interpersonal connections. Persons who know narcissistic people often characterize them as attempting to impress others by boasting and putting others down. Those that deal with narcissists think them competent and beautiful. Therefore their activities are initially effective. Over time, these partners, however, develop an attitude of hostility toward the narcissist.

Numerous studies have found that narcissists rely on their relationships with others to make them feel good about themselves. They appeal to others' admiration and attention in order to maintain favorable self-images that are readily endangered. Furthermore, they are continuously on the lookout for even the tiniest sign of disrespect.

Narcissistic abuse is not widely understood, yet it is extremely prevalent. So many people suffering from it are suffering in silence. The pattern of psychological neglect and invalidation that its victims face is difficult to recognize and even more difficult to reconcile. Narcissism – why is it not good for us? How is it hurting our lives, our hearts, our souls, our world? It is everywhere. It is almost as though something has seeped into the water supply. It is making everyone sick. Many people say, I do not have something like this in my life. Oh, yes, you do. Even if it is not targeting you directly, simply look on a social media feed and you will see this. It is a problem all over the world.

But people are finally beginning to understand what they have been dealing with. They are learning about narcissistic personality disorder and traits of narcissism. And having a clear grasp of the situation helps you deal with it. Understanding allows one to cope with it.

But there is also a pattern of grief. Some people might have spent 10 weeks, 10 months, 10 years, 25 years trying to change a narcissistic person in their life. And then they finally see the pattern for what it is.

This book is all about narcissistic abuse, which can go beyond just romantic relationships. It can be suffered at the hands of friends, family, bosses, etc.

Narcissists tend to be very resentful and angry. They feel like the world is not fair, like life was never right to them; they often walk around with a victim mentality. So what is the difference between someone who has narcissistic traits, and someone who has a narcissistic personality disorder? This comes down to a technical issue. Whenever we talk about disorders in the medical circle, one of the key issues is that the person is experiencing either some impairment or distress due to their behaviors or symptoms. A classic example would be a depressed person who has irregular sleep; they feel sad, cannot concentrate, and feel worthless; they are uncomfortable. And on top of that, it is probably causing them problems at work in their relationships in their lives. All of us have sad days. But when it begins to affect our lives on multiple levels, we diagnose it as major depressive disorder.

When it comes to narcissistic personality disorder, things can get tricky. Many people with these patterns have no impairment. They are getting promotions, and they are getting the girl or the guy. Everyone thinks they are so cool. They are often very financially successful. So, where are the impairments and distress? They would say 'I do not have any problem. It is your problem. It is their problem. It is the world's problem.' They defend themselves. They rationalize everything they compartmentalize; the world almost exists for their convenience. So, they are not distressed. And depending on what index you use, they are not impaired either.

To understand, let's return to the concept of narcissistic abuse. Narcissistic abuse is not a well-articulated phenomenon. Those of us who do talk about it have not even come up with a standardized definition. But, to me, it is a pattern of psychological neglect. Invalidation in dehumanization causes significant stress or psychological harm or distress to the subject of such abuse. And this abuse is characterized by chronic invalidation, lack of compassion, lack of respect, lack of what we call mutuality, and a sort of cold indifference on the part of the narcissist to the other person.

People on the receiving end of narcissistic abuse are full of self-doubt and anxiety; they do not feel good about themselves. They worry a lot. They feel hopeless, and they feel helpless more than anything else. And all those patterns make them less efficient and less able to manage their day-to-day lives. It hurts their relationships; it hurts them at school. It hurts them at work. So, if anything, while the narcissistic people are not experiencing distress and impairment, the people who are experiencing their abuse are. So why do they do this to people they say they love and care about?

The truth is that their love is very superficial. It lacks the depth that a healthy intimate relationship has; it tends to be what we call very instrumental, and, in that way, narcissists view human relationships as conveniences. Consider the following thought process: 'Right now, I like this cup, because it will give me what I want to drink. Okay, very convenient. I am quite focused on it now; but in 10 minutes, I will not give this cup a second thought because I will not need it.' That is how narcissists treat people. Think they love merely means paying the rent, buying you gifts, taking you out to dinner. I took you on vacation, I came to your sister's wedding, what more do you want from me? And so, as far as they are concerned, that is love. For a narcissist, their relationships are often quite transactional.

CHAPTER 2: DIFFERENT TYPES OF NARCISSISM

Narcissism is a personality characteristic that comes in a variety of shapes and sizes. However, there is just one diagnosis for this issue in terms of mental health.

"What does it mean to be narcissistic?" is a legitimate question. However, is the term "narcissism" being used too loosely, or are there multiple types?

You may have observed that phrases like "narcissist" and "narcissism" are becoming increasingly common. In addition, it is not uncommon to see lists of "renowned narcissists."

Anyone can probably think of at least one person they know who matches this description. However, these labels carry a lot of baggage and carry many connotations. As a result, it is essential to grasp their true meaning and manifestation.

Characteristic narcissism versus narcissistic personality disorder:

When individuals discuss narcissism, they may refer to it as a personality trait or a mental illness (NPD).

Typically, narcissism is diagnosed as NPD when it becomes more than just a personality feature and interferes with many aspects of life. Narcissism may manifest in various ways, even in those who have a formal diagnosis, and that is what we will discuss here.

In general, Narcissism is linked to the following characteristics:

- An excessive emphasis on oneself

- An exaggerated perception of one's importance

- A strong need for praise and attention

However, when it comes to various varieties of narcissism, psychologists have identified the following:

- overt narcissism

- covert narcissism

- antagonistic narcissism

- communal narcissism

- malignant narcissism

Another way to look at narcissism is to consider how it interferes with your daily activities and your capacity to build connections.

Narcissism can be adaptive (beneficial) or maladaptive any given situation (unhelpful).

Research reveals that narcissism may be classified as mild, moderate, or severe, depending on the individual. In this case, it is logical to believe the various "forms" of narcissism lie somewhere along the same continuum.

A more in-depth examination of narcissistic personality types can help us better comprehend the mental processes, emotional responses, and behavioral patterns associated with narcissism.

Adaptive versus maladaptive narcissism

Some studies distinguish between healthy and unhealthy forms of narcissism. This demonstrates the contrast between narcissistic traits that are useful and those that are destructive.

Adaptive narcissism refers to traits that may be beneficial including strong self-esteem, self-reliance, and the capacity to appreciate oneself. Unlike maladaptive narcissism, adaptive narcissism does not diminish as we age.

Maladaptive narcissism is associated with character flaws that do not serve you and can harm your relationships with others and yourself. It encompasses traits like entitlement, violence, and taking advantage of others. NPD-related symptoms might include some of these.

The maladaptive form of Narcissism is usually the form that is referred to when people discuss Narcissism.

Both adaptive and maladaptive narcissism can be inherited through genes and shaped by early life experiences.

Overt narcissism

Narcissism is also known as grandiose narcissism and agentic narcissism.

Overt narcissists might be described as extroverted, arrogant, entitled, and overbearing, with an overinflated sense of self requiring praise and admiration, as well as an inability to empathize.

According to some studies, extraversion, and openness – two of the Big Five personality qualities – are linked to overt narcissism.

Overt narcissists are more likely to be satisfied with their lives and less likely to feel unhappy, worried, or lonely. They may also have an inflated sense of self-worth and intelligence. According to a 2018 study, narcissistic people may also overestimate their emotional intelligence. Overt narcissism, according to certain studies, is a kind of hostile narcissism. Therefore, there is an emphasis on rivalry and competitiveness.

Covert narcissism

This is the opposite of overt narcissism and is also known as vulnerable narcissism or secret narcissism. Contrary to popular belief, those with covert narcissism do not exhibit the same characteristics as those with overt narcissism.

The following are characteristics of someone who is hiding their narcissism:

- signs of poor self-esteem expressed in words or action

- increased risk of anxiety, sadness, and self-loathing

- introversion

- uncertainty or a lack of faith

- defensiveness

- avoidance

- a tendency to feel or act like a victim

The self-centeredness of someone with covert narcissism is likely to clash with a profound dread or feeling of not being enough.

A research paper in 2017 looked at personality and covert narcissism and discovered that it was most closely associated with high levels of neuroticism (the predisposition to feel unpleasant emotions) and disagreeableness.

Someone who suffers from hidden narcissism may find it difficult to take criticism. They have the inclination to internalize criticism, or take it in a harsher manner than what was intended.

Covert and overt narcissism are not always exclusive. A person with overt narcissism may go through phases where they display more covert characteristics.

Hostile/Antagonistic narcissism

Antagonistic narcissism includes the following characteristics:

- arrogance

- a predisposition to exploit one's position

- competitiveness

- a tendency to quarrel or to get into disagreements

People with antagonistic narcissism are less likely to forgive others than those with other varieties of narcissism. Researchers believe that people with hostile narcissism are also less likely to trust other people.

Communal narcissism

A different type of overt narcissism is communal narcissism, which is often viewed as the antithesis of hostile narcissism.

According to a study issued in 2018, people who suffer from communal narcissism have high standards for justice and believe they are selfless. However, their actions do not coincide with their ideals.

Those who are affected by communal narcissism may exhibit the following characteristics:

- get easily incensed by moral issues

- identify as kind and benevolent

- respond vehemently when they perceive an injustice

So what distinguishes communal narcissism from real care for others' well-being?

People with communal narcissism have a strong sense of social power and self-importance. They may feel they have a strong moral code or care about other people, even though their behavior may contradict these views.

Malignant narcissism

When it comes to narcissism, there are many degrees of severity. Malignant narcissism is the most extreme.

Malignant narcissism is characterized by several narcissistic characteristics, such as a great desire for admiration and a sense of superiority over others. It might manifest as:

- vindictiveness

- sadism (the practice of taking pleasure in other people's suffering)

- abrasiveness in social interactions

- hypervigilance in the face of hazards, or paranoia

Sufferers are prone to have problems with the law or with substance abuse, and often struggle to control their anxiety and improve their day-to-day functioning.

In short

When someone has narcissism as a personality feature or as a personality disorder, it can complicate relationships. Overt, hidden, communal, hostile, and malignant forms of narcissism impact how you view yourself and interact with others.

Many persons with narcissism do not see the need to change, which makes treatment challenging. But living with narcissism can negatively impact mental health, causing anxiety, depression, and drug abuse.

The good news is that if someone suffering from narcissism symptoms decides to seek help, there is much room for improvement and progress.

CHAPTER 3: BEING IN A ROMANTIC RELATIONSHIP WITH A PERSON WHO HAS NARCISSISTIC TRAITS

Loving a narcissist is simple at first. They do not get bored easily and are often physically handsome, personable, and sexually alluring to men and women alike. In addition, we are pulled to someone because of their personality traits such as brilliance, charisma, exceptional skills, and professional accomplishments.

However, when dating a narcissist, it would be best if you never presumed that your partner shares your views. Even though some narcissists desire long-term relationships, most are skilled gamblers, especially those who have never been married. According to them, "the chase is preferable to catch." Their goal is to be admired and have their sexual desires satisfied while putting in as little effort as possible. Relationships are just transactions. They want to be able to satisfy their demands by having a variety of solutions available. They look around at other people while they are in a relationship and even flirt with you while they are doing it!

Despite their lack of empathy, narcissists have a high level of emotional intelligence, which allows them to comprehend, sense, express, and control their emotions. As a result, they often become more skilled manipulators. To attain their goals, they use dishonesty, sometimes purposefully and sometimes out of habit. They can even think they are being sincere when they are not. Even though they are emotionally unavailable and self-centered, they might be kind and decent listeners at first. By disclosing private and sensitive information, they make themselves look more vulnerable. This is a seduction technique tactic. Fawning, flattery, and subtlety are all part of their arsenal.

Women who are narcissists are charming and seductive because of their physical attractiveness and sexual allure. Afterward, they engage in a game of cat and mouse with the males to arouse their jealousy or get them to pursue them. Manipulative acts of seduction by male narcissists include providing extravagant presents, excellent cuisine, and an upmarket way of life. Love-bombing is a narcissistic technique in which a person bombards their partner with attention, verbal statements of "love," physical affection, and material possessions. After that, they go missing.

The narcissist is the center of attention when dating

At the beginning of a relationship, we tend to romanticize our partner. But idealization can feed our rejection of warning signs like loneliness, depression, or codependency. When we fall in love, it is only natural that we want to spend as much time as possible with our beloved. So, when a guy or woman plans a great evening, we are delighted to go along with it.

Be aware that a narcissist's relationship evolves according to their rules. Compromise is a painful loss of power to them, while we aim to satisfy them. They may become defensive and claim to be doing everything for us, even though they do not even ask what we want. With their desire to be in charge, narcissists soon gain control over our schedules, where we go, what we do, and even whom we spend our time with. We go along at first because we want to be with them, but subsequently, because we are afraid. This is especially dangerous for codependents who readily give up on themselves, their friends, and their hobbies when entering new partnerships.

Non-objection to the narcissist's decisions and viewpoints is a trait of codependency. For fear of upsetting our new partner, we may withhold information that might harm the relationship in

the beginning. We do not informing him or her of the consequences of their actions. As a result, they have no or very little
motivation to alter their behavior. In a perverse way, codependents and narcissists are made for one other.

Things to pay attention to

We fall in love with somebody for their wonderful traits, not
their flaws, but if we are in a relationship with a person with
narcissist traits, they will not be able to keep their real colors
hidden for long.

When people learn more about narcissism and themselves –
even those who claim their spouse changed drastically after the
wedding – they confess that there were early warning flags that
they ignored. As an illustration, narcissists can come across as
brash and arrogant. They are also known to suffer fits of rage.
Disagreements of any size can swiftly escalate into a full-blown
war. They are unwilling to accept accountability. Every little
thing is due to someone else's mistakes, even our own. Pay
attention to whether they criticize their ex, seem entitled, or are
uncaring, manipulative, or disrespectful to others, even if they
treat you well.

Assume you will be the victim of narcissistic abuse at some
point in the relationship. Recognize narcissistic abuse when you
see it.

When it comes to dating, be on the lookout for red flags and blind spots. At first, we are intrigued by their accomplishments and stories, as well as their witty banter. As the talk progresses, it becomes increasingly apparent that the focus is solely on them. Listening well is a valuable skill, but it is doubly so when dealing with a narcissist.

Some narcissists are dogmatic in their belief that they are better than everyone else. Therefore, they must always be correct and will not accept dissenting views. If we are honest with ourselves, we can see that they do not appear to care about us other than to satisfy their sexual and emotional desires. Look for signs that interaction with them has sapped your energy, and left you feeling ignored, invisible, patronized, or tired.

Narcissists will degrade their partners to feel better about themselves if they can no longer maintain their superior status through charm and bragging. They find something wrong with us or give us advice on how we should behave, dress, eat, or alter our diet in some manner. They criticize us constantly.

The hardest people to deal with are perfectionistic narcissists. A narcissistic woman, for example, could try to change her man's appearance and tell him what to wear.

Narcissistic people will accuse us of being overly sensitive if we communicate our pain. If we have been mistreated in the past or have poor self-esteem, we may first ignore criticism presented playfully or gently. With time, degrading statements become more common, overt, and insensitive.

Severe narcissists may probe us about our other connections and chats with family, therapists, and friends. They may try to restrict our social relationships and activities by requiring us to dress and behave in a specific manner.

Empathy is absent from the personality of a real narcissist. Our feelings and wants are dismissed as inconsequential, and we become depressed. If our spouse does not display appropriate emotional responses when discussing something sad or essential to us, it may indicate a lack of empathy. We may ask ourselves if a narcissist is even capable of love.

The characteristics of codependency make it difficult for codependents to identify warning indicators while in a relationship with a narcissist. For example, if you are still in love with your abuser, leaving may be tough. In this case, it might be because we were raised by an abusive or narcissistic parent who did not respect our needs or feelings. Healing our codependency will enable us to alter these dynamic relationships to receive authentic love.

CHAPTER 4: NARCISSISTIC MIND GAMES

Narcissistic Abuse Syndrome occurs when a person is in a relationship with someone who has a Narcissistic Personality Disorder (NPD). Abusers use various techniques to exploit, brainwash, set up, soothe, break, and eliminate victims. The victim continues to give up her power to her abusers. By attacking the victim's character and vulnerability, this abuse attempts to isolate and discredit the victim before moving on to blame those who may have viewed things differently. Love bombing is a narcissist's method of cementing the attachment and confusing the target. Other narcissist techniques include devaluation, isolation, trauma bonding, cohesive control, projection, stonewalling, cliff-hanging, and mind control. After that, they will start employing mind control techniques, such as gaslighting.

Psychological games are being played. It involves put-downs that are both subtle and overt. Triangulation. Gaslighting. Projection. Sadly, they are strategies that malignant narcissist survivors are all too familiar with. They have lived in a battle zone, suffering from an abuse cycle of love-bombing and devaluation—psychological violence on steroids, as the perpetrators of narcissistic abuse are seldom held accountable.

Narcissistic abuse has the drawback of going mostly unreported and unrecognized, thus the victims get little help. Most manipulators are skilled at managing their victims' perceptions; all we know about a scenario will be taken away from us and turned around to make matters worse. These genuinely broken narcissistic individuals fail to recognize the humanity of others who stand in their way.

There are a variety of abuse strategies used to keep the target on the straight and narrow. These include contradicting, constant shaming, invalidation, framing, double binds, and undermining. The narcissist will at different times both pacify the victim and force her to lose her grip on reality.

When the victim refuses to bend to the manipulator's will, the abuse becomes more severe. It gets worse if the victim refuses to cooperate. It is impossible to avoid the perception that an apology implies an admission of guilt. Abusers are excellent at establishing double binds and trapping victims in an endless cycle of pleasing them and reading their minds. There is no way out for the victim. Nothing but laying down in helpless surrender. You will also get the impression that you have done or said nothing properly. This will immobilize most targets, causing them to retreat in order to appease the unrelenting abusers who shame, humiliate, and criticize. As long as you give in to the demands of a manipulator, they will take advantage of you with no remorse. They relish taking advantage of others while vehemently denying doing so.

True manipulators can anticipate the actions of their targets and use that information to their advantage. Their shortcomings are also harnessed and used against them to cast doubt on the person's character. In this kind of abuse, the victim is subjected to a series of manipulations to conceal their genuine identity and replace it with a false one. Narcissistic abuse often involves the perpetrator isolating and discrediting the true victim through character assassination and other means. A common assertion made by those who manipulate you is that even others in your immediate circle agree with them; however, this is false.

Narcissistic abusers are masters of image management and can successfully persuade others that they are great members of society and exceptionally remarkable individuals. They will come after you if you see through any of this and begin to call them out on what they have done to you. Unless you are ready to play very dirty, have no pity, or put aside all humility and disregard their sentiments (as they have yours), you cannot win when dealing with them. They do not follow the same set of rules as most people. Even if you do this, you will feel a great deal of sorrow for sinking to such levels. Most individuals who attempt to match the narcissist end up turning on themselves and renouncing their basic values.

Also keep in mind that narcissists keep tabs on everything you do. They pay attention to what you say and reflect your behavior back to you. They do not foster interpersonal relationships or have any sense of responsibility. They are gathering data; they collect and retain whatever information they think they can use against you. They have a lot of common sense. They pay attention to your actions and body language. They keep tabs on your activities and routines. They are on a mission to inflict harm on their prey.

If you find yourself as a target of one of these psychopaths, I strongly advise you to leave the relationship as soon as possible. They have created a fantasy world for themselves, so they will never have to face up to who they really are. Because they believe in their distrusting and slightly delusional reality, they specialize in misquoting you and adding their own "unique twist" to chats and text messages. It is like they pick and choose the facts they want to include in their story to make it seem as though they are the victim instead of you.

The demonization of an individual or group is at the core of malignant narcissism. Their paranoid beliefs and egotistical narrative will be the filters through which all information is viewed. Pity is usually used as a pretext for starting a slander campaign. They will do all in their power to steal your identity and convince people that you are something you're not. This identity is then believed not only by the victim, who has slowly and steadily lost their minds due to gaslighting, trauma bonding, isolation, and covert put-downs, but also by the abusers.

The anger of targets who get irate and frustrated from the constant barrage of allegations will be used to convince others that the true abuser is the target. The victim, of course, will be likely unaware of what is going on, thus the target has no means to protect themselves in the event of an attack. Narcissists want to be the best. Thus this provides them a boost of confidence and self-control. When you do or say something that challenges their reality or what they believe to be true, a narcissist sees you as an adversary.

Targets who have empathy and self-reflection will undoubtedly begin to question if the abusive manipulators are correct, as narcissistic sociopaths have mastered the art of preying on our brains. For the manipulative abuser(s) to establish a convincing case against their victim, whatever perceived or real faults the target has will be noted and documented. Narcissistic abusers like instilling doubt and distrust in the minds of those they target. If your ideas and reasons do not match theirs, you are considered foolish and disrespectful.

Narcissistic abusers seek to obtain material from their prey to create a warped narrative that portrays them as perfect while painting you as "the issue." You merely have to recite your lines from the script to provide them the information they need to build up a tale about you on their own. As a result, the manipulative abusers' self-aggrandizing narratives are reinforced, and it is the only role they feel comfortable playing. People subjected to narcissistic abuse tend to over-apologize, over-admit, or even admit doing something they do not remember doing. We find ourselves apologizing, even if we had no intention of doing so. Because of this, targets are far more exposed to assault and exploitation. Anyone might crack and turn on themselves under the psychological strain and gaslighting they are subjected to. Abusers aspire to destroy their victim by insinuating abuse and then erasing all traces of it. They want their prey to be on their hands and knees before them.

When it comes to cheating, lying, withholding, and manipulating, narcissists have no issues. However, if you do any of those things to them, they will take offense. The goal always justifies the means for a narcissist. If we grow a backbone and call them out on anything, they will be extremely angry and attempt vengeance by ensuring that people's perceptions of you are warped. Experts at foreseeing outcomes, they will devise clever framing schemes to thwart their victims. That way, no one will ever believe or hear what the victim has to say.

Narcissists are always putting themselves in a position of strength so that they may strike when it is most advantageous. The most common narcissistic lie is that they care for or love us. Nothing the narcissist does is motivated by unconditional love, but rather by a desire to play the innocent faithful ones, while the victim is held responsible for their suffering. A person with paranoid delusions does not accept responsibility for their fears, lacks respect for their target, and is unable to negotiate in good faith. They also suffer from pathological jealousy and have an unusually distorted view of reality. They have a twisted explanation for and justification for everything, and they will not allow anyone to hold them accountable for that explanation. Their goal is to cause further humiliation of their victim, who has already hit rock bottom, due to the abuse cycle.

If you have been the prey of narcissistic abuse, you have nothing to be ashamed of. You are not to blame. Unlike your abuser, you are able to own up to your blunders. You can admit your flaws. You are open to hearing what your abuser(s) has to say and trying to comprehend their point of view. You can see through their crap, methods of control, and manipulation. Unfortunately, these positive traits do not protect you from the narcissistic predators that live in your midst. This form of abuse teaches us to despise ourselves not only for our vulnerabilities and shortcomings but also for our strengths, which manipulators will exploit against us.

Keep in mind that is merely a game for them to win, and you were unfortunate enough to be caught up in it before realizing what you were doing. You most likely have a charming personality and were taken advantage of by people who lacked morals or values. Be kind to yourself and accept responsibility for your actions. You must forgive yourself for becoming a different person to fend off the assault. Forgive those who will never "get it" or who have not stood up for you, since only a person who has been through it can genuinely understand what you are going through. Even though you will never forget what it was like to be abused, forgiving our manipulative abusers is essential to recover truly. If we do not do this, the pain and trauma will keep replaying in our minds and bodies.

CHAPTER 5: THE IMPACT OF NARCISSISTIC ABUSE

Narcissistic abuse can have far-reaching and long-lasting effects, regardless of how long you have been a victim. As well as destroying our self-esteem, narcissistic abuse may also wreck our personality and alter our core identities. Below, we discuss a number of consequences of narcissistic abuse:

Deterioration of confidence

Narcissistic abuse has many effects on our personalities, but the most significant one is the deterioration of confidence. Narcissists need to undermine our self-esteem to silence any critical thinking on our part and erode our personal limits. It is easier to see through narcissist tactics when you realize your value. You will also be more willing to speak up for yourself and about the things you need.

Internalization

Does you tend to take on the problems of the entire world instead of taking care of yourself? If so, narcissistic abuse is likely to blame. Narcissistic abuse can devastate a person's previously confident demeanor, leaving them filled with self-blame and an almost unbearable sense of worthlessness. Narcissists make us assume responsibility for their blunders as well as life's inevitable tragedies. In the long run, this (together with our diminished self-esteem) results in someone who is continuously sacrificing themselves on the altar of self-blame.

Anxiety and depression after a traumatic experience (PTSD)

Some people believe that PTSD exclusively affects veterans or individuals who have suffered a great deal of physical trauma, yet this could not be further from reality. An incident or occurrence that fundamentally and severely destabilizes our sense of self or our beliefs might result in Post-Traumatic Stress Disorder (PTSD). This is exactly what narcissistic abuse does, and it may leave us depleted and dejected once it is over.

Insecure attachment in relationships

Due to the destabilizing nature of narcissistic abuse, it can have a major influence on our ability to connect and attach to people, and our outlook on life and relationships. When we feel that falling in love or opening up to someone is not safe, it is called insecure attachment. As a result, we either avoid connection, grow concerned about it, or utilize a combination of the two, making our relationships explosive and flammable. In addition, long-term abuse distorts your worldview and attitude, making you more cynical and scared of the outside world.

Increased display of narcissism

When narcissists surround us, it is hard to avoid developing our own narcissistic characteristics. Humans are social animals that tend to imitate the actions of those around them. The more time you spend in a narcissistic society, the more likely you will embrace it as a normal and appropriate way of life and communication. Thus, you may begin to show your own narcissistic traits, as well as lose your capacity for compassion for others.

Superficiality

Living with or loving a narcissist necessitates a certain level of superficiality, which may seep into our personality. When dealing with narcissists, it is impossible to be upfront and honest about your feelings. Even if you do not mean it, you must put on a grin and seem like you are pleased and involved in order to avoid rejection. Then it becomes the norm to fake emotions you do not feel and go along with decisions you completely disagree with.

Impaired communication abilities

Even if you were an outgoing or sociable person before dating a narcissist, you might find it difficult to speak as openly and efficiently as you used to. This is because when you have been the victim of narcissistic abuse, it is unsafe for you to express yourself or open up and discuss your feelings or values. This impairs your ability to communicate, and as a result, your friendships, attitude, and even your general personality may suffer.

Repeated emotional trauma leads to PTSD and C-PTSD, which should be enough of a reason to leave an abusive spouse. But, for the most part, the hippocampus, which is the part of the brain responsible for memory and learning, shrinks, as repeated emotional traumas increase the amygdala, which contains basic emotions like fear and sadness.

Basics of the hippocampus

The hippocampus is located in each of the two temporal lobes. It aids memory storage and release. The hippocampus plays a critical role in short-term memory, which refers to the ability to remember information for a brief time before either transferring it to long-term storage or forgetting it completely. A person's ability to learn is heavily reliant on short-term memory.

In addition, one of several analyses that have been carried out yields quite troubling conclusions. Corresponding to a study by researchers from the University of New Orleans and Stanford University, patients with higher baseline cortisol (a stress hormone) and more PTSD symptoms had the biggest losses in hippocampus volume over time.

The more time you spend with an emotionally abusive spouse, the more damage your hippocampus will sustain. In addition, victims of narcissistic and psychopathic abuse may experience confusion, cognitive dissonance, and abuse amnesia due to this neurological process.

Basics of the amygdala

Narcissists inflict persistent worry and terror on their victims, causing the amygdala to fire. The amygdala is in charge of basic emotions like love, hatred, fear, lust, and vital life processes like breathing and heart rate. It is also in charge of the fight-or-flight response. Victims of narcissistic abuse experience this regularly, often for long periods. The amygdala retains memories of what we felt, saw, and heard after a traumatic incident. Any subliminal cues of such stressful situations will set off the organs' attack or escape pattern, resulting in avoidance behaviors or emotional unrest (another good reason to refrain from stalking your ex on social media).

Even after a toxic relationship has ended, victims can still experience PTSD, C-PTSD, panic attacks, phobias, and other symptoms owing to their hyperactive amygdala. As a result, victims of narcissistic abuse often resort to rudimentary self-defense methods like the following:

- Use of denial to avoid confronting difficult emotions or aspects of their lives they do not want to accept.

- Compartmentalization. Victims compartmentalize the abusive components of the relationship so they may concentrate on the good parts.

- Projection. A victim's compassion, empathy, care, and understanding are projected onto their abuser while the abuser does not have those characteristics.

Narcissistic abuse alters your brain's structure and functioning in unexpected ways.

The hippocampus is where the brain makes new neurons and connects them to others (Goleman, 2006). Cortisol damages the hippocampus, which puts it at risk of long-term emotional suffering. Continual stress alters the pace at which neurons are added to or removed from the hippocampus, due to the presence of cortisol. When cortisol attacks the neurons, the hippocampus shrinks and loses neurons. Cortisol, according to Goleman, activates the amygdala while impairing the hippocampus, causing us to focus on our emotions while limiting our capacity to learn new things. In other words, when we let stress or resentment take over our thoughts, our mental agility starts to splutter.

Similarly, when we are depressed, our prefrontal brain activity decreases, and we have fewer thoughts. Sadness and extreme anxiety and rage both increase brain activity beyond what is normally considered safe.

Though things may look bleak, there is some hope. It is possible to repair your hippocampus and stop your amygdala from hijacking your psyche by engaging in reparative activities which we will discuss later in the book.

PART 2 - BREAK UP WITH A NARCISSIST

CHAPTER 6: BREAKING THE CYCLE

I t is tough to break up with a narcissist.

The narcissist may decide to depart after being triggered by something. For one of you, this is generally a life-changing experience. The narcissist may choose to leave if you are ill, incompetent, or reluctant to participate in the life they have planned for you. If it demands the narcissist to be more accountable and emotionally involved, even something good like having a child might break the delicate equilibrium of your relationship. It is possible that the narcissist might also depart the relationship if they became ill, grew older, lost their job, or got promoted.

You can expect certain things when you break up with a narcissist, regardless of who initiated it:

They are going to hold it against you.

Whenever things do not go as planned, the narcissist places all the blame on another party. They think the relationship is over because of you. They might believe you are overweight, needy, or unreliable, so they make fun of you for it. They will try to lead you to believe you have messed everything up, damaged the relationship, and shattered their faith in you in the process. You are ungrateful for what they have done. Without them, you would be nothing. You have wiped out all the two of you have worked so hard to achieve. You are an arrogant jerk who puts others before yourself. The narcissist's life has just been a whole lot more miserable since you entered it.

Of course, this is upsetting, disrespectful, utterly unjust, and incorrect. At this stage, the narcissist will no longer consider or listen to you, and they may not even be willing to speak to you. If you sincerely repent and plead for reconciliation, you may be reunited for a short time, but the relationship between the two of you will never be the same again.

They will convincingly suggest that you have made a mistake.

Having your decisions devalued by the narcissist for months or years may cause you to doubt your judgment. You can be sure that the narcissist will do everything in his power to persuade you that you have made a blunder. They will use charm, convincing, intimidation, goading, and direct provocation to regain control of the relationship.

The narcissist will state something along the lines of, "You just misunderstood what I was trying to communicate. You should be aware that I genuinely care about you, so why do you need me to reiterate it so frequently? Are there no memories of fun occasions we have shared? You spend an excessive amount of time dwelling on the bad aspects of life. You have no idea how anxious I have been recently. You are far too sensitive about stuff. You are acting irrationally. You tend to become too sentimental."

Recognize that all of his "reasons" are negative statements about you and what is wrong with what you are doing, so do not listen to his words. They are not sincere appeals to stay in the relationship; they are psychological tactics designed to undermine your self-esteem.

To make you feel awful about yourself, the narcissist will use persuasive tactics such as: "Before you married me, you were nothing. Return to your pathetic family and let yourself rot. You will regret it when I am living it up in California. I am confident that I will meet someone who genuinely loves and values me."

They will use guilt to persuade you to stay.

For the narcissist, using guilt to entice you back into the relationship is a highly effective strategy. Whenever they do anything kind for you, they will bring it up or underline how much they care about you, or remind you of the fantastic experiences you have had together. Narcissists resort to devaluation assaults if positive reinforcement fails to win you back. They will answer your complaints against them. They blame their partners for the behaviors they are engaging in at the time, such as yelling, name-calling, hostile conduct, and selfishness, hate, and passive-aggressiveness.

For a caregiver, being accused of being selfish, nasty, cruel, or hurting someone's feelings may be very upsetting. The fact that those actions and sentiments exist makes you feel mistreated. You strive so hard to avoid doing or being those things. These remarks are very telling of the narcissist's lack of understanding and acceptance of you as a person.

If the narcissist accuses you of something, you are more likely to feel guilty, which will lead you to work harder to establish your innocence. Because this brings you back into the relationship, the narcissist loves it. Until they are ready to quit the relationship, they might keep you feeling powerless, guilty, and engaged in it until it suits them otherwise.

They will continue to make demands for attention even after you have ended things.

Leaving will be much simpler if you can avoid any further interaction with a narcissist once you have broken up. Narcissists can be quite persistent when trying to get your attention. When they feel rejected, they engage in all sorts of behaviors to attract attention, such as drunken calls in the middle of the night, "accidentally" breaking into your home to retrieve their belongings, dozens of texts or emails per day, and repeated requests to "explain" why you left — all of which lead the narcissist to accuse you of being negative.

These cries for attention might go on and on if you have many children. After seeing her ex-husband, one client became so nervous and choked up that she could not speak. The man was so desperate to get her attention that he even pushed the court to "order" her to communicate with him "for the sake of the children." But, of course, he just did it because he wanted to be noticed for his selfish needs.

They will commit to improving themselves.

Once you have resisted persuasion, guilt, and attention-getting activities, the narcissist will use the promise of change to entice you back into the relationship. At this point, the narcissist appears to comprehend your distress and your desire to leave suddenly. These individuals appear to be taking ownership of their actions and admitting mistakes. They may go to treatment, do all you ask of them, and go about things according to your instructions. They sincerely apologize for any inconvenience this has caused you.

For a caregiver who is sincere about wanting the relationship to work, this is an enticing argument. This time, it appears that the narcissist has grasped what you have been trying to communicate and is ready to make things right with you again. Moreover, they seem to be earnest in their intentions. Sighing with relief, you feel a renewed sense of optimism.

This hope will inevitably come to naught. Narcissists will never let you be free of their control, and they are unable to restrain their impulses for long periods. Things may appear to be improving for a time. It is important to remember that when narcissistic people feel secure in their relationships, they often revert to their old behaviors, such as being self-absorbed, careless, arrogant, and unfeeling. Similarly, every time something goes wrong, they immediately revert to their old protective and aggressive behavior patterns. You must decide how many times you will trust the narcissist's lies.

They will use slander and defamation to harm others.

If your relationship ends because of a narcissist, it is not easy to keep it private since your ex-partner will expect everyone you know to pick sides. They will spread the word about your split as quickly as possible, both in person and on social media, to your friends, neighbors, church members, and club acquaintances. Most caregivers find this quite upsetting. The narcissist insisted on complete secrecy regarding your interactions during your relationship, and now they are spreading lies and slander about you to harm your reputation. Unfortunately, caretakers frequently stick to their word and refuse to bring up the subject of the relationship, allowing the narcissist to continue lying with impunity.

Gossip is a manipulative strategy to make you look awful and to garner sympathy for the narcissist as much as possible. Additionally, it has the potential to put you back under their control by re-engaging you with them.

They may engage in stalking.

Narcissist stalking is not always overt or violent. It is not uncommon for one to appear at the grocery store just as you are about to depart, to show up at a community or social event you are attending, or to alter their running route so that they pass your house every morning. So prepare yourself in advance in case these unplanned meetings arise. They are put in place to keep you on edge and constantly aware of the narcissist's presence.

They will express their desperation.

Even while narcissists portray themselves as powerful and self-reliant, their true nature is one of severe dependency. It may be hard for you to stop caring for the narcissist. As a result of your previous caregiving, you may receive calls from them needing your assistance with something ranging from fixing a car to completing their bookkeeping, taking down their Christmas decorations, or keeping their dental appointments, all of which require your time and attention. Refusing these incessant pleas might be taxing and tough for you to do. As a result, you are dragged back into encounters with the narcissist much too often, and it is not in your best interest.

Missing your narcissist is nothing out of the ordinary.

The subject of "Why I Miss My Narcissist" is quite intriguing for many people.

They ask, "Why would I miss someone who has treated me so terribly, who has rejected and undervalued me? How could I have ignored something so obvious? Because of them, I have turned into a deranged codependent."

The issue with narcissistic relationships is the length of time it takes to establish them in the first place. After thinking about them, ruminating on them, and attempting to solve things and address the disagreements, it amounts to a full-time job in its own right. However, even though it was an unproductive period, you may find yourself not knowing how to spend all the free time you now have on your hands, and missing it as you might miss a former job.

Euphoric recollection is a component of it as well. One of the biggest problems with these kinds of relationships is that you only remember the good times. You recollect that one very memorable night out on the town where the hotel clerk surprised you with a bottle of wine, but you fail to remember the quarrel you had earlier in the day, or the fact that he was messaging the person he was cheating on you with later that night. You are cherry-picking all the excellent moments using euphoric recall, in any case. You tend to overlook the fact that that one night was part of a much larger pattern of invalidation, abuse and gaslighting.

Trauma bonding may also be a factor in your longing for your narcissist. People from narcissistic families are particularly vulnerable to trauma bonding since these interactions suggest a problematic relationship from your past, generally with your parents. When the narcissistic connection is lost, it is almost as though you are doing more than simply breaking up with your partner. It is as if you are unraveling a maze of horrific memories from your upbringing. As a result, you have the sensation that something is yanking on your skin. It is a grueling experience.

It is normal to crave certain things while you are missing them, and your brain may be affected by these addictive cycles. You yearn for them and long for them to satisfy your cravings.

Sometimes, believing that ending the relationship was a victory is difficult to comprehend. You may find yourself wondering if perhaps you were in the wrong all along. You revert to your old ways of deceiving yourself and accepting the narcissist's propaganda as gospel. If you find yourself thinking this way, making a list is essential. Write down all the negative things you experienced during your relationship and force yourself to look at it regularly. Do you long for the days of being duped? Do you long for the days when you were deemed ineligible? Do you long for the days when you were treated like a second-class citizen? Do you long for the days of being deceived? Once you realize exactly what it is you are craving, you will be relieved to be free of it. If necessary, stick this list to the bathroom mirror to remind yourself that you are relieved it is all over.

CHAPTER 7: ESTABLISH HEALTHY BOUNDARIES

Narcissists have little regard for the consequences of their behavior on others. They view individuals as resources to be exploited. As a result, it is critical to set up clear limits with them upfront. Here are several practical methods to get the job done:

Do not try to defend, justify, or explain yourself. Narcissists put others in doubt about their abilities or motives. They get a boost of confidence and a sense of control when they do this.

The freedom to determine what you share with others is an important part of creating boundaries. Narcissists are more likely to use your personal information against you if you cannot keep it to yourself.

An intruding narcissist does not require you to defend your ideas, feelings, or behaviors. Saying something like, "I hear your perspective, and I will consider it," might help defuse a narcissistic attack. If your activities are being questioned, tell them you are confident in your decision. "That is personal," or "We will simply have to agree to disagree," will do if they insist on an explanation.

Exiting a damaging encounter does not need consent from anybody. What is healthy for you is up to you to decide, not someone else.

Glancing at your watch and saying, "Look at the time, I am late," is acceptable. After that, you should depart. What are you running late for? It makes no difference. Being in the company of controlling or abusive behavior makes it more difficult to prioritize self-care when you are already behind schedule.

Use your cellphone as a prop if you have one. "I am sorry, I have to take this call," is an acceptable response. After that, you should depart. Alternatively, plan how much time you will offer a narcissist and set the alarm on your phone or watch for when it is time. Exit the room when the alarm goes off.

You might also face bad treatment head-on by stating something like, "I am going to excuse myself. This is not healthy. Let us speak about it another time when you are ready for a productive dialogue. This type of conversation is not for me."

Choose what you are willing to put up with and what you are not. Healthy boundaries include knowing when to say no. Decide what you are ready to accept from others and what you are not before taking anything from anyone else. For instance, you could be fine with friendly banter but not with sarcasm. Having strong beliefs is one thing but hurling insults and bullying is another.

As an example, say, "If you continue to use profanity and insults in our chat, I will terminate it until you show me some respect." You are not required to go into any further detail at this point. If a narcissist persists in his or her violent conduct, either leave the room or hang up the telephone. Do not interact with them again, no matter what they say or do.

Narcissistic people may go through various behaviors in response to boundaries you set, such as blaming you, diminishing your feelings, acting the victim, claiming you are overly sensitive or becoming enraged. Even though such techniques are upsetting, ensure your boundaries are unassailable.

Develop the ability to skirt awkward queries or critical remarks deftly. For example, politicians avoid unpleasant questions from journalists by quickly changing topics.

Similarly, when confronted with an intruding inquiry from a narcissist, you have the option to change the subject politely. Change the subject to something the narcissist enjoys discussing. See if you can elicit their advice on having a success-ful relationship or making a difficult decision in your work or finances. Even if their answers are full of clichés, they will talk about themselves instead of you in their responses. You never know, you could even get some inspiration. Being able to change the subject of a conversation deftly is also gratifying.

Take the bully down by the scruff of the neck. Narcissists are driven by a deep-seated need to be seen and validated, which helps them cope with feelings of worthlessness and emptiness. Because of this, they are always trying new things to see what they can get away with.

Calling out what they are doing is one method to deal with this. Say something like, "Are you trying to make me feel awful or put me down?" Or, "I have noticed that whenever I begin to speak, you interrupt me." Speak matter-of-factly about such matters. Don't allow yourself to be affected by the narcissist's response. Simply allow yourself to be happy with the knowledge that you have named what is taking place and then move on.

Beware of narcissism's influence. Remember that narcissists have dedicated their whole lives to devaluing and exploiting others for their own gain. Narcissistic people tend to have erro-neous perceptions of the world and others, as well as themselves.

In situations where you fail to set effective boundaries, show yourself compassion. Then, next time, decide what you will do differently. Setting boundaries is a continuous process.

When setting limits, do not forget to incorporate penalties. Setting limits includes understanding what you will do if those boundaries are not followed. The greatest way to deal with consequences is to have them crystal clear in your mind before you act. Then, when a barrier is crossed, take prompt and decisive action based on your selected consequence every time. You risk losing credibility if you do not do so.

CHAPTER 8: NAVIGATING A DIVORCE COURT WITH A NARCISSIST

Most people will do almost anything to avoid going to court, especially over a divorce. We dread the financial costs, the loss of private life and antagonism between you and your spouse, the pain it causes children and other family members, and the fear of entrusting your life to an unknown stranger sitting on a bench in front of a courtroom. (Not to mention the cautionary tales in movies as well as the horror stories you have heard on the news or from friends.)

Despite the media attention paid to divorce cases that go to trial, especially when one or both parties are wealthy or famous, just 5% of divorces wind up in court. Approximately 95% of couples resolve their differences amicably or use approaches like negotiation or collaborative divorce to limit the harm and financial expenses of the divorce.

Although there are some facts to bear in mind, I have avoided using the pronouns he or she to avoid being accused of prejudice.

The first is that males outnumber women two to one at the end of the narcissistic continuum (for the sake of simplicity, we will refer to them as "narcissists"). Yes, two times as many. This gender discrepancy is mostly due to men's tendency to be more aggressive than women — and, unlike women, they are often encouraged to flaunt the exploitative, entitled behaviors that define narcissistic personality disorder.

Secondly, women initiate 60-69% of all divorces in the United States; this has been true historically since the 19th century, and it continues to be so now, even due to the fact that divorce lowers women's living standards while raising men's, and men are more inclined to remarry than women. Researchers in law, psychology, and sociology have all been curious as to why this is the case.

According to research published in the *American Law and Economics Review* by Margaret Brinig and Douglas Adams, women are more likely than males to file for divorce when child custody is a factor. If the woman knows she will receive half of the marital property, alimony if she is eligible, and child support, it may be wiser to dissolve the marriage than stay with a spendthrift or an authoritarian with money issues.

Stanford sociology professor Michael Rosenfeld looked at some of the causes for why spouses are likely to start divorce proceedings:

It has been proven that marriage is a factory for conventional gender expectations because women still shoulder two-thirds of the domestic tasks. Eventually, there is a power imbalance between the sexes. In addition, women are more sensitive to relationship troubles, which makes them more unsatisfied.

He discovered no gender difference in initiating breakups between cohabiting and non-cohabiting couples; both parties were equally inclined to call it quits. However, comparatively speaking, 32% of cohabiting couples and 36% of non-cohabiting couples said that the choice to break up was mutual, compared to 19% of marriages.

Women initiating the divorce often do so as a result of the marriage being gendered. Nonetheless, if someone files first to jump-start discussions, it does not always indicate that they want to wind up before a judge.

Let us start with why the narcissist is quite likely to wind up in court, despite the fact that any reasonable person would be very motivated to avoid it.

Even if there are no actual "winners" in divorce, the duties and assets can be distributed fairly; that is not the narcissist's point of view. Whatever the facts are, this person is likely to believe that they are victims and will not meet in the middle, so forget about negotiating or mediation. The narcissist's ultimate objective is to be proven correct, and he or she will do everything to achieve that goal.

"One of my clients was married to someone who had three relationships throughout the length of the marriage and often spent their holiday money on affairs," a lawyer said. "While writing long begging letters asking, 'Why are you doing this to me?' to the judge, the narcissist sought to persuade him that his spouse was the one having an affair (which she was not). Truth is not simply relative to narcissists; for many people, it is absolute."

Keeping people off-balance is a narcissist's relationship pattern, and going to court will not change that. Even the family court system may be used to their advantage. An extraverted, charismatic type with plenty of cash on hand might be particularly dangerous. For example, they are prone to filing countless papers with baseless (false) allegations of 'neglectful parenting,' which waste everyone's time and resources. It is usually an attempt to exhaust you.

Irregular empathy is a common feature of pathological narcissism; here, it manifests as complete disdain for the potential harm the narcissist's actions might do to others, particularly his spouse and children. Narcissists do not think about other people because they are preoccupied with themselves; nothing else matters except meeting their demands and desires.

When faced with a difficult circumstance like divorce, our fear of hurting other people, what they will think of our actions, and how it will influence our future relationships are what keep most of us on the upfront and narrow. But not the narcissist, you understand. Instead, they follow what military strategists refer to as a scorched-earth doctrine, in which nothing is left in his or her wake. Sadly, this includes the narcissist's children, who end up being used as bargaining chips in their game of chess.

The narcissist is still manipulating you by involving you in a legal struggle. To self-regulate, narcissists want relationships, and dragging you through the court will provide them with an exhilarating rush of power and control. But, of course, the narcissist has to find a new needy victim as soon as you are gone. The narcissist has no interest in putting the stress of divorce and all the accompanying negotiations and give-and-take that goes along with it behind them, making dealing with one all the more difficult.

The narcissist requires a tangible trophy, which you may pro-vide him or her by packing up your belongings and leaving. The narcissist gets a rush from defeating others, and court battles are typically fought as battles of attrition.

The narcissist's impact on the divorce process

If you are in a court of law, it is because he or she will not talk about terms on a fair basis. If the narcissist goes to court and the judge decides, it may be easier for him or her to avoid taking responsibility for the outcome, especially if it is not good. The narcissist does not want to give up voluntarily, and the judicial system tells him or her that winning or losing is not his or her responsibility. Ceding control paradoxically allows the narcissist to keep up the façade of power. This procedure may also comprise the following elements:

Obstructionist tactics

Family court processes can take a long time depending on where you reside, and the narcissist will tell his or her lawyer to consume as much of it as possible. Be ready for several motions to be filed, demands for further time and delays, and so-called "emergencies." Whatever the case, the narcissist will portray themselves as the victim. The narcissist solely accepts his or her truth, regardless of whether or not others find it credible. Narcissists may even be willing to lie in sworn documents.

Delaying when gets under your skin, not showing up for court dates, adding false information in files and appeals that have to be addressed, and not releasing material completely are all strategies that may be used by the other side.

The court is often likely to trust the narcissist's account since he is skilled at self-presentation (and believes in his superiority). The ruse may also succeed if the other person is affluent and well-known (and you are not).

Refusal to enter into negotiations or come to an agreement.

The narcissist understands that the longer the procedure takes, the more easily he or she will be able to manipulate and pressure you. That is what he or she is banking on. Kirkpatrick claims that narcissists are by nature competitive: "When negotiating a settlement with a narcissist, certain tendencies emerge. They make unsatisfactory proposals, such as lowball ones or ones that are offensive. As a result, there are always bargaining chips available to stall the discussion or start over from scratch, and they fail to respond to the issues raised. There will be no honest exchanges of goods or services." As a result, they cannot reach a compromise and will likely maintain the same viewpoint notwithstanding changes in the facts and circumstances."

Painting you a dark shade of gray

Whatever Jell-O or mud is on hand will be tossed to see what clings to the wall, whether true or not. The narcissist's lack of empathy, lack of concern for the relational repercussions, and determination to win at all costs mean that you should expect to be smeared in the paperwork, court, and society at large. It will take more time and money to defend or rectify these papers, opening the door to the judge believing the narcissist. As Kirkpatrick points out, it is characteristic of the narcissist to spread his or her tale to new or old friends, family members, coworkers, and individuals affiliated with your business or profession to pollute the waters, destroy your reputation, and gain support for oneself while doing so.

Continually returning to court, even if you have settled your case.

Due to everything said above, the narcissist will continue to use the judicial system to settle any legitimate disagreements and to instigate new ones as long as possible. The narcissist, as previously said, manipulates the system. There are no limits, especially when it comes to children. Not sharing calendars, appointments, or itineraries, signing up children for activities that fall on both parents' time without prior notification and discussion, when the parent does not have the legal power to do so, are quite normal following a high-conflict divorce. Invading a child's privacy to get psychiatric data is another offense, as is not paying payments on time.

As the narcissist is well aware, these things might turn into legal disputes that need to be settled through the courts, which is important to keep in mind. These are only guidelines that you should go through with your lawyer. It is usually a good idea to seek out the services of a therapist to help you cope with the psychological toll that going through a disputed divorce has on you. A therapist is not your lawyer, and an attorney is not your counselor; keep this in mind while working with either.

The following are a few strategies to keep in mind when facing a narcissist in divorce court:

1. Make sure your lawyer has a strategy for dealing with the patterns of behavior of your soon-to-be-ex. Also, watch carefully to determine whether your ex is operating on his or her behalf, or with an attorney. If your lawyer does not have the skill and experience to deal with people like this, you will either need to find a new one or be quite firm in your instructions to the lawyer on how to enforce limits.

2. Save copies of everything, especially receipts for purchases. If you have never been one for keeping meticulous records, now is the time to start. Consider gathering as much evidence as you can if this case becomes a "he said/she said" dispute. This is vitally significant; many people have used it to refute the falsehoods of their ex-partner in court.

3. Remain calm and avoid falling victim to their traps. Do not vent your rage via voicemail or by sending threatening or degrading emails or messages, particularly if minors are involved. The most valuable thing to remember is to keep your mouth

and pen under control. If you have had a bad ex, be aware that they may modify your messages and emails before sharing them with others in his new tight circle. Because of their poor self-esteem and need to be seen as 'the nice guy or gal,' narcissists must maintain control over their stories. Keep an eye out for the narcissist's manipulations, and try your best not to be sucked in. Do not criticize your partner in front of your children or among the individuals he associates with. This will only inflame the situation further. Keep the high path in mind, even if your spouse is abusing the children. Your children will be grateful. At some point, they will realize their narcissistic parent's accusations are nothing more than a ruse to gain control. Thus, the narcissist is doomed to fail in the game of life. If you simply keep focused on the next appropriate move, they minimize themselves.

Heightened stress, and issues with trust and security are all very real consequences of these divorces. However, your chances of surviving will improve if you are both legally and mentally prepared.

CHAPTER 9: HOW TO ADDRESS A JUDGE EFFECTIVELY IN COURT

You are in court with a narcissist, and it seems like everyone believes him or her all the time. Do you feel helpless? Hopefully, by the conclusion of this chapter, you will have figured out how to bring the narcissist to justice.

When you are facing a narcissist in court, it can feel like they constantly have the upper hand. They are in this habit of attempting to make you seem terrible while making themselves look good. In addition, they plan to love bombing everyone in the system, from judges to lawyers to the custody evaluator. And they will do all in their power to paint you as the villain. They may even be submitting fraudulent motions. Many decent parents have been accused of being abusers, unsuitable, drug addicts, or having other vile characteristics by their exes.

And as you sit there contemplating, you ask yourself, "How are they getting away with this?"

One thing to bear in mind is that only the court has the authority to compel someone to do something.

"My lawyer has done nothing to regulate him, or his behavior," is a common complaint heard from clients. However, keep in mind that a lawyer has no other option except to file a document with the appropriate court. Once you have submitted your motion, you will be able to appear before a court. The narcissist can then be exposed.

So what should you do to ensure your success? Firstly, in court, never use the term "narcissist." You will have other options to hold the narcissist accountable for their actions. And you must go about it in an organized manner. You will have to put together paperwork and exhibits that methodically demonstrate that a defendant is a horrible person, and you must do so as per the legislation.

It is also necessary to provide summaries, for example, of instances in which the person involved lied, accompanied by all of your supporting material. Then, make a list every time they failed to pick up the kids or arrived late or spoke ill of you. That sort of thing. You may also have a slew of text messages informing the children that one of their parents is an alcoholic or negligent and does not want them around. These can be fantastic trial evidence. However, continue to adhere to the rules outlined in the law.

Consequently, you are providing the court with something they can keep, something they can utilize when enforcing the law, something which will deliver you the outcomes you desire. Simply stating, "That individual is a narcissist" will not be enough. It does not help you achieve anything. You do not expose them in this manner. The only way to show who they are is to systematically use your information and put it together according to legislation.

Keep in mind that one of their goals is to win over the judge and jury's hearts. So your goal is to get power by identifying who in the system they would most likely respect – this is likely to be the judge – and then use that information to gain leverage that might expose them for what they are. This is going to be a crucial part of the equation.

Many individuals believe that no one ever gets to a narcissist, or manages to get them to compromise. However, this could not be further from the truth. It is possible to win your case if you threaten a supply source that is more significant to them than the supply they gain by yanking you around the system.

Four approaches to sway the court in your favor

- Never lie before a judge. If you do so, they will become

enraged, and you will lose that case, motion, or hearing.

- Your attorney has an ethical obligation to represent you in court and also should not lie to the judge, any of the parties, or deposing counsel.

- Do not interrupt a judge while he or she is speaking. As soon as they begin speaking, everyone in the room should remain silent.

- Judges do not like disorganized people. Organize all your papers and proof when asked by the judge to present.

CHAPTER 10: BREAK OFF COMMUNICATION

To shut off communication with a narcissist, the **no contact rule** is used. We must break off all communication with them and avoid confronting them at all costs.

Keep in mind the following:

- Refuse to communicate with the narcissist in any way, including texting or sending an email.

- It is important to put up barriers such as blocking the narcissist's contact information, avoiding returning calls from unfamiliar numbers, or changing your phone number altogether if required.

- Deactivate your social media accounts if you are concerned that the narcissist may still find a way to follow you or that you will continue to check their profile.

- Update your passwords.

- It is best to break ties with anyone who cannot see behind the narcissist's front.

- Keep your personal information hidden from people you intend to see in the future (to prevent the narcissist from learning anything about you) and not allow them to tell you anything about the narcissist.

- Keep your distance from the narcissist and try not to go near their home, job, or other places they frequently visit.

Even though you have done all of this, the narcissist may still try to contact you. They might show up in front of your house, school, or place of business without warning. They might bring you presents or flowers to keep you on the receiving end of their abuse. Strive to stick to the no contact rule. You may be able to obtain a restraining order if required.

When I initially heard about the no contact rule, I thought it was extreme and pointless. As I pondered this, I asked myself, "Why should we eliminate someone from our lives? In light of all the common interests we once had, shouldn't we be able to at least greet each other when we see cross paths?" Pretending that someone did not exist struck me as very juvenile. However, all of these ideas were brought on because I was still ignoring the systemic emotional and psychological abuse I had endured.

Why does the no contact rule need to be in place?

Breaking up with a narcissist is very different from breaking up with someone who is emotionally healthy. Departing with your head held high is a risky proposition. Unlike other people, narcissists are unable to accept a breakup. Instead, they will do whatever they can to retain you as a selfish nourishment source for themselves.

How might they react?

They can put on a decent and attentive partner act all over again in an attempt to win you back. They might express their love and affection for you and their inability to function without you. They might make hollow promises and reminisce about simpler times. Expect some thoughtful presents and flattering remarks.

If you find yourself in a scenario like this, keep in mind that things will return to normal after the threat of losing you has passed. Furthermore, no matter how fantastic one feels during the idealization phase, it appears superficial, fake, and even aggressive if one takes a step back and looks at the situation objectively.

There is also a possibility that they will make you feel guilty.

Their memories of your faults (or blunders to them) and good deeds can serve as a powerful motivator. They might tell you that you are selfish, that you are taking them for granted, and that you will never find another person like them again. Depending on how we feel about being accused, we may react in a variety of ways.

- We are capable of displaying empathy, so we might accept that they have a point and do our best to accept some responsibilities.

- We may believe we have been falsely accused, and strive to defend ourselves.

- We may become enraged and act violently when this happens.

In the end, it will not matter how we handle these charges; it will only benefit the narcissist. There is no such thing as a good or terrible reaction to a narcissist. Either way, they will realize that they still have power over us and can sway our emotions and ideas in their direction. Therefore, we must maintain our composure and resist the temptation to protect ourselves.

Slander and emotional blackmail are two other tactics the narcissist may use. They may even start gossiping about you behind your back to ensure that no one believes a word you say.

Keep your cool once more. Do not let other people's views sway your decision-making process. Your sanity depends on following the no contact rule!

It is also possible that they may disregard you completely.

Even though this is a remote possibility, they may not care if they lose you. They may argue that you did not deserve them in the first place. Then, once they have terminated things with you, they might go about bragging about how they ended the relationship or start flaunting their new love life with someone else.

This is actually the most fortunate conclusion, despite how bothersome it may appear to be at first glance.

How cutting ties with the narcissist might make you feel...

Other psychological and spiritual difficulties may arise from being in a narcissistic relationship, such as trauma bonding, fear of being alone or abandoned, and a lack of self-confidence or self-love. Cutting the narcissist out of your life totally might seem tough at first, considering the trauma bonding between you two. To begin with, you may doubt and question yourself regularly, and you may feel compelled to give them another chance to alleviate your concern. To keep the no contact rule in place, strive to resist the impulse to visit them again. Stay away from those who do not understand your circumstances and surround yourself with people you can trust throughout this crucial period. On top of that, you may compile a list of all the mistreatment, lies, and abuse you have endured and refer to it whenever you doubt yourself. Understanding narcissistic abuse and manipulation can help you understand your struggle in a new light.

How long should we discontinue contact with the narcissist?

Forever!

We do not use the no contact rule to exact vengeance on the narcissist, to make them suffer, to compel them to change or miss us, or regret what they have done to us. We do it to protect ourselves from further abuse. In addition, following the no contact rule does not imply that you have fully recovered from your traumas.

The primary objective is to identify the weaknesses that made us vulnerable to narcissists in the first place so we do not go through the same trauma and suffering again. The ultimate objective is to clear our minds of the toxins, shield ourselves against narcissistic abuse, and take back control of our lives.

PART 3
- CO-PARENTING
ADVICE

CHAPTER 11: DISCUSSING DIVORCE WITH YOUR CHILD

Divorce and Children

As a youngster, a divorce or separation may be a very difficult period. However, there are a number of strategies to assist your children in adjusting.

Everyone engaged in a divorce or separation goes through many ups and downs, but children in particular frequently feel as if their entire world has been flipped on its head. The disintegration of a parent-child relationship at any age can be difficult to bear.

Kids might be in a state of shock, confusion, or even anger. They may even feel responsible for their family's difficulties. During a divorce, you will experience a great deal of sorrow and pain, however, you may greatly alleviate your children's suffering by prioritizing their well-being. Help your children become accustomed to new situations by being patient, reassuring, and listening. If you provide them with regular routines, your children will know they can depend on you for stability, structure, and care. The stress and sorrow of viewing parents in conflict can be avoided by having a functioning relationship with your ex. With your help, your children can not only get through this difficult period, but they can also come out of it stronger, more confident, and closer to both of their parents than they were before.

What your child wants from you and your ex-spouse during a divorce.

- The two of you must always be a part of my life. So please always get in touch with me through phone, email, or text message. When you do not stay connected, I get the impression that you do not care about me or that you do not truly love me.

- Please quit arguing and try to get along with one other instead. On my behalf, try to agree. In the midst of your disagreements with each other, I begin to question whether or not I have done something wrong.

- I want to spend time with you both and love you both equally. If you show any signs of jealousy or resentment, I feel as though I must choose one parent over the other and love him or her more.

- Please speak directly with each other rather than relying on me to pass messages back and forth.

- Please refrain from saying anything negative about my other parent in front of me.

- I would like to have you both in my life. Mom and Dad are the people I turn to when I need guidance or assistance.

How to explain divorce to children

When it comes to notifying your children about your divorce, many parents get paralyzed with fear. However, you and your children will both benefit from having a plan of action in place before you sit down for a chat. You will be more prepared to assist your children in dealing with the news if you can anticipate difficult questions, deal with your fears, and plan carefully what you will be telling them.

When and how to say what you want to say

If you can, try to use an empathic tone and focus on the most crucial things at the beginning of your message. Then, give your kids the benefit of the doubt by providing them with an honest yet kid-friendly explanation of why things are the way they are.

Honesty is best.

A lengthy explanation of why you are divorcing may only confuse your children. So instead, you may start with something straightforward and honest, such as "We are no longer friends." While parents and their children may not always get along, they do not divorce or stop loving each other. You may need to tell your children this.

Speak your heart out.

Let your children know that your love for them has not changed, no matter how basic it may sound. Your children will still be taken care of in every manner, from making breakfast to assisting with homework. By conceding that some things will change and others will not, you can manage your children's inquiries about how their lives will alter. Reassure them that you have each other's backs and that you can handle anything that comes up.

Avoid blaming others.

As parents, it is important to tell your children the truth, but without criticizing your spouse. A little diplomacy might help you avoid playing the blame game when there have been terrible occurrences, such as adultery.

- Make a united statement. A pre-divorce explanation

should be agreed upon and adhered to as much as possible.

- Organize your thoughts before you speak. Prepare ahead of time for a conversation with your children about potential changes in their living situation.

- Show moderation, and do not overdo it. When citing the grounds for the breakup, be considerate of your spouse's feelings.

Exactly how much information should I tell my child about the divorce?

To begin with, you will have to decide how much information to provide about the breakup or divorce and how much to keep from them. Consider how a certain piece of information will influence them before sharing it.

- Be mindful of age. In general, smaller children require less information and are best served by a straightforward explanation, but older children may want more information. Inform them about the logistics. While informing your children about any changes in their living situation, school, or activities, do not overload them with information.

- Keep it real... No matter how much you have decided

to tell your children, keep in mind that the information should always be accurate.

- When a parent and spouse divorce, it might feel like the death of a loved one, the loss of the family, or just the loss of the life they knew before the divorce. Emotional support can help your children cope with their loss and adapt to their new surroundings.

- Listen. Encourage your youngster to open up, and listen to their thoughts and feelings. They may be experiencing feelings of grief, loss, or irritation that you did not anticipate.

- Help them express their thoughts and emotions. As a youngster, it is natural to be unable to communicate your feelings. Support them by paying attention to their feelings and encouraging them to express themselves.

- Allow them to be truthful. Children may be reluctant to express their actual sentiments for fear of harming you. Let them know they may say whatever they want. They may blame the divorce on you, but they will have a tougher time healing if they cannot express their true thoughts.

Divorce should be a constant topic of conversation.

In the course of a child's maturation and understanding of the world, they may have new questions, sentiments, or worries regarding what happened. Of course, let them know you appreciate them. However, even when you cannot address their concerns or make them happy, you need to address them rather than reject them. You may also build trust by demonstrating that you have a grasp of the subject matter.

Kids need to recognize that they are not to blame for the divorce. As a parent, you may assist your children in dispelling this myth by doing the following:

- Clarify the facts. Explain why you divorced. And be patient as they come to their own understanding. One day they may appear to "get it," but they may be doubtful the next. Your child's misconceptions and perplexity should be handled with care.

- Reassure. As often as necessary, reassure your children that they are not to blame for the divorce and that both parents will keep on loving them no matter what.

Children have an incredible capacity for healing if given the proper support and compassion. However, to convince your children that you will always be there for them, you need to be consistent in your actions and words.

There will always be two sets of parents in attendance. Your children can still have good, loving connections with both of their parents, even if they are no longer living under the same roof.

- Tell them it is going to be OK. Of course, things will not always be simple, but you should tell your children that it will work out in the end.

- You may reassure your child of your love by hugging, patting them on the shoulder, or simply being in the same room as them.

- Honesty is the best policy. Respond genuinely to any fears or anxieties that your children may have. If you do not know how to reply, say softly, "I do not know right now, but I will find out."

- Maintain a sense of normalcy during the divorce. While it is beneficial for children to adapt, adapting to several different situations at once may be quite challenging. Provide your children with as much consistency and structure as possible to help them adapt to change.

- Remember that maintaining structure and regularity does not need a strict plan or an identical routine for both parents. However, establishing regular home routines and continuously informing your children of what to anticipate will help them feel peaceful and secure.

- Routines give a sense of security, strength, and stability. When children know what is coming next, they feel more comfortable. After supper comes homework and a bath, which may put a child's mind at ease even if they move to a new house. Maintaining a regular schedule also entails adhering to your children's rules, incentives, and punishment. Discipline kids through a divorce by keeping restrictions and making sure they do not go against them.

Care for your body and mind.

You must first put the oxygen mask on yourself before putting it on your child in the event of an airline emergency. Similarly, when supporting your children during a divorce, the most important thing to remember is to first look after your own well-being.

Divorce or breakup can be difficult to deal with. It can cause a wide range of distressing and disorienting feelings. Mourning the loss of a relationship can be accompanied by feelings of isolation and anxiety. Learning healthy strategies to deal with the grief of divorce or separation will help you remain calm and make your children feel more at peace.

Eat well and get plenty of exercises. Stress and frustration are frequent in divorce, and exercising helps alleviate them. When it comes to eating healthily, cooking at home is more time-consuming than going out, but it is worth it in the long run.

Social life

The more often you see your friends and family, the better. While it may be tempting to isolate yourself and avoid talking about the divorce with friends and family, obtaining face-to-face support from others is essential for helping you cope with the stress of a divorce. If you do not want to talk about your split, they will respect your wishes.

Keep a diary.

Keeping a diary is a good habit. The act of writing down your thoughts, opinions, feelings, and moods might help you overcome feelings of depression and rage. Also, you will be able to track your progress in retrospect as time passes.

Seek assistance.

When it comes to divorce, at the absolute least, it is a difficult and emotionally draining process. Get help from others to ensure you do not strike out at your children with bitterness, rage, or frustration. Talk to friends or a support group face-to-face. It is never too late to make new acquaintances if you have ignored your social group while married and do not feel like you have anybody to confide in.

Be aware of your emotions towards your child.

It would be best if you never expressed your negative emotions towards your child. Keep your child out of the conversation. Keep chuckling to yourself. Stress may be relieved, and anger and unhappiness can be averted if you and your children can laugh and play as frequently as possible. Get help from a therapist. Find a mental health expert to help you deal with extreme feelings of anger, fear, sadness, humiliation, or guilt. Work together with your ex-partner. Separated or not, parental conflict can be detrimental to a child's well-being. You must avoid putting your children in the center of your conflicts or making them feel like they must select between you and your spouse. Following these pointers can help your children avoid much pain in the future.

In-person or over the phone, never quarrel in front of your children. If necessary, reschedule or end the conversation with your ex. Use etiquette. Do not discuss the other parent's actions with your children. If you do not have anything good to say, do not say anything at all. This is the oldest law in the book. Be a gentleman and a lady.

Conversations with your ex

Maintain a professional demeanor when conversing with your ex-spouse. This not only sets a wonderful example for your children but also encourages your ex to be gracious in response. Rather than focusing on the negative aspects of your ex, choose to focus on their virtues. Put some effort into it. The sooner you can establish a friendly connection with your ex-spouse, the better. Children can be comforted and taught problem-solving skills by watching their parents be pleasant to each other. Resolve issues with your ex-spouse over child custody. Take a breather and think about the bigger picture. In the long run, what is best for your children? Maintaining healthy ties with both parents throughout their life. Think ahead so that you can remain calm. Your children's physical and mental well-being, and your own independence, are long-term goals. Consider the well-being of everyone.

After a divorce, it is essential to focus on what is most important in your new life: the well-being of everyone involved, especially your children. Some children have a relatively easy time coping with divorce, while others have a far more traumatic experience. Professional help may be necessary if your children continue to struggle. Grievances are common once a split occurs. Following a divorce, children are likely to experience the following emotions, which are all perfectly normal:

- Anger. Your children may vent their hatred and animosity toward you and your spouse for causing them to lose their sense of normalcy.

- Anxiety. When faced with major life events, it is normal for youngsters to experience anxiety.

- Depression. If the family's new position has left them feeling hopeless and powerless, they may suffer from a moderate type of depression.

Your children's adjustment to the separation or divorce will take some time, but should gradually improve.

If your child continues to experience sadness, anxiety, or rage, it is a sign they could benefit from more assistance. Pay attention to the following warning symptoms:

- Unrest at night

- Lack of focus

- Problems in the classroom

- Addiction to drugs or alcohol

- Eating disorders

- Self-injury or cutting

- Outbursts of rage, or violence

Divorce-related warning flags should be discussed with your kid's doctor, teachers, or child psychotherapist.

CHAPTER 12: HOW TO ANSWER YOUR CHILD'S QUESTIONS ABOUT DIVORCE

Divorce infuriates children in a variety of ways. "Why did you and Daddy divorce?" may be a common question for younger children. When did you stop loving Mommy?" The children of divorced couples may say, "Daddy stated it was your fault that you divorced. What have you done?" It is not strange for parents to be surprised by their children's inquiries regarding divorce at the most inconvenient times. Make plans now! If you do not understand why children ask these questions and be prepared with useful replies, you might unwittingly make problems worse. To aid you, here are some tips.

Why is the child so curious?

Divorce may be a confusing time for children.

They may hear their parent on the phone ranting about the other parent or overhear a conversation concerning one of their parents having an extramarital relationship. Or they may witness you arguing at a shop or in the street. Their loved ones are at odds with one another, which causes a great deal of stress on their part. Fear and insecurity ensue as a result. "Why do you no longer care about Daddy?" or "Was there an affair?" are common questions kids ask.

Because they are asking certain questions, it may appear as though they are looking for those answers. However, they are asking because they do not know how to ask for what they need. For example, "I am feeling incredibly uncomfortable and anxious about myself during this divorce and need reassurance that I will be fine."

In an attempt to find out whether or not they will be all right, they are contemplating the information they are aware of. They do not really want to know about your co-parent's affair or whether you love Mommy or Daddy or not. Adult topics that are too complex for them to comprehend will exacerbate the situation.

Pay attention to how they feel instead of what they are saying.

If they are nervous or afraid, let them know you understand. Assure them that everything will be well; they deserve that assurance. If they ask you a question about adult issues, tell them that it is not relevant to them and that everything will be OK. Even though life might be frightening, you will all get through it. Hug them. Making an emotional connection with them is essential to making them feel secure.

Children are not miniature grown-ups.

Even if your youngster is really intelligent, they are not old enough to hear about adult things. This also holds true for teens. Intelligence is frequently mistaken for maturity by parents. A person's brain does not reach its full potential until the age of 25. Your youngster will be under a lot of stress and strain if you expect them to grasp adult issues. Do not force youngsters into the role of grown-ups.

Connection

Connection is the most important factors in a child's sense of security. Words are not always required. Hug them regularly. Remember, it is not just about what you say; it is about how connected you are to one other. Sure, you are free to express yourself. Tell them it is difficult. Tell them that things will improve. Those remarks, however, will be worthless if they are not accompanied by genuine affection.

Do not respond immediately.

Breathe deeply. You are under no need to respond straight away!

In our society, people often reply swiftly to one other. We do not take the time to think about the question properly and why the person is asking it. When your youngster raises a question, pause for a few seconds and take a deep breath. Consider why they posed the question. You will be better prepared if you know what prompted the query in the first place. Saying "I need some time to think about this before responding" is quite acceptable.

Practice mindfulness

When it comes to connecting with your children, practicing mindfulness may be a lifesaver.

Empathize with their emotions

Parenting can be challenging. It hurts us when they are hurting, and we want to make their pain go away. But ignoring the feelings of a child when attempting to address their inquiries regarding divorce is a bad idea. Learn to empathize with their emotions. Do not solve anything too quickly.

Your side of the story

When your child asks you a question about the divorce, please do not take it as an opportunity to present your side of the story.

You could think, "Well since they are asking, I will tell them about the affair."

But putting children in the center of a debate puts them at risk. It is a subtle way of urging people to see things from your point of view. Co-parents have varying viewpoints, and asking your children to determine which one is correct makes them more uneasy. Trying to understand whose point of view is "superior" is pointless. Always avoid putting your children in a position where they have to figure out who is to blame.

Do not make the other parent a bad example.

Do not use your co-parent as an example of bad behavior. This is not how children learn. It makes them nervous to hear about the horrible things their other parent is doing.

I am not implying that you support criminal activity. Nor am I proposing you sugarcoat anything that you cannot genuinely excuse. Keep in mind that your kid is unhappy and that their concerns regarding divorce stem from that distress. Telling your child how terrible their other parent is will not make things better. Connection is what they need to feel better. In addition, if you want to instill positive values and conduct in your children, you must lead by example.

Find out what the child wants.

Asking yourself what your child REALLY wants to know is a valuable skill. Remove yourself from the literal context of the question and seek to understand its emotional underpinnings. Keep in mind that the most often asked question is "Am I OK?"

CHAPTER 13: DEVELOPMENT AND ADAPTATION OF CHILDREN AMIDST PARENTAL SEPARATION

Much of a child's psychological maturity occurs in the context of the connection between an adult and a youngster. If a child is separated from or loses their parents because of separation or loss, their cognitive, psychological and physical development will likely be affected. When a kid can live in an atmosphere that is supportive of the mourning process and can explain and comprehend his life experiences, the negative impact of parental separation/loss can be lessened to some extent. Conversely, children who have experienced this trauma and have not gotten adequate assistance in addressing loss concerns often remain "stuck" at the age of the loss of their major attachment objects.

Separation and loss in the first year of life

The child's feeling of security and trust in the presence of adults is eroded.

- Parents and caregivers need to be accessible "on-demand" for the newborn, so they can once again support the child's developmental demands.

- Every encounter with a newborn should be assessed by asking the question, "What will assist this baby learn to trust that adults will be available?"

- For these newborns, maintaining a regular schedule is critical.

A newborn whose dependence requirements are not addressed will grow up believing that life owes him, which is not a healthy outlook on life for anyone. He may have a difficult time managing the requirements of others in the future. Trust in other people will be eroded. Even if they do not show up until the fourth or sixth grade, learning difficulties owing to difficulties with cause and effect might arise.

During the toddler years (Ages 1 – 3)

In the short term,

There will be an imbalance in the amount of dependency and independence suitable for a given age.

When the family's position changes, the child's ego may be upset. Internal and external stimuli may dull the child's sense of awareness, and the most recently learned abilities are likely to be lost.

Parental loss can disrupt a child's ability to learn a new language, particularly if that parent was the child's "interpreter."

Care must be taken to address the child's dependence demands while at the same time allowing him to feel sufficient and independent on his own terms.

If the youngster is permitted to return to previous levels of functioning, they are likely to learn the abilities within a few months.

Long-term issues are more probable if the kid is put under undue pressure to perform at a high level or learn new abilities without adequate transition or reattachment.

In such cases, the individual may permanently assume the role of victim or perpetrator. In the long run, there may be significant control concerns. The interruption of ego development may increase "borderline personality" disorders. The lack of self-awareness may be a constant problem. There may be long-term linguistic difficulties. In adulthood, these people may be stiff, inflexible, and unable to control their violent impulses in an acceptable way.

Loss and separation during the early years of education (Ages 3 - 6)

Because of his selfish magical thinking, the youngster may misinterpret the reasons for the separation and loss.

As adults, we must try to understand the child's thinking concerning the loss. Is he blaming himself for the loss? Is he certain that he can reverse it?

There may be a conflict in the child's thoughts regarding the "good" and "bad" features.

You must know how to minimize the impact of your loss. For example, identifying, clarifying, and correcting the magical thinking. In addition, adequate chances for play must be offered, as at this age, all psychological difficulties, including grief, are healed largely via play.

Because of the Oedipal struggle and the kid's magical thinking, he or she may think that the loss resulted from the child desiring the opposite sex parent all to himself. In terms of sexual identity, this might have long-term consequences. In circumstances of sexual assault, this might be magnified. There may be a tendency for a youngster to blame the loss on either being "too large" or "too small" in his family because of the magical thinking and "big vs. tiny" battle.

The child's energy levels may be lower in the short term while he goes through the mourning process. In addition, disagreements with peers can arise when school-age youngsters become increasingly aware of their differences from their classmates.

Provide the kid with periods when he can focus on mourning, to then allow focus on the activities at hand, whether academic or peer-oriented.

Assist the youngster in expanding his or her knowledge of losses by providing him or her with accurate facts.

During adolescence

- The teenager may confront and reject parental figures who are still present.

- Adolescents need to feel that they are becoming more in charge of their own life. It is also important to give children authority over other elements of their life while they are going through a difficult phase such as a parental divorce.

- They need to be involved in the decision-making

process for their future.

Grieving the loss of early relationships may be difficult for adolescents. Yet, because they need to recognize formation and establish a sense of self-worth, they require as much knowledge about their early past as is accessible.

When it comes to selecting how much of their past to share with close friends and family, teenagers often need guidance.

It is common for adolescents to feel suicidal or to engage in antisocial behavior if they believe they have no control over their lives.

CHAPTER 14: RECOGNIZING PARENTAL ALIENATION SYNDROME

Child psychiatrist Richard Gardner coined the term Parental Alienation Syndrome (PAS) in 1985 to describe a child's conduct that he felt to be characterized by excessive but unfounded fear, disdain, or anger toward a parent. Child custody litigation can be used to diagnose psychological manipulation or undue influence by one parent on a child, often by the other, who may be trying to prevent a continuous relationship between the child and the other family members following family separation or divorce.

Gardner was the first to characterize a distinct symptom of a parent trying to remove their child from the other parent as punishment or as a part of a divorce. The child's campaign of condemnation against the parent, which has no basis, is the principal expression. It is caused by the child's participation in demonizing their estranged parent, along with the alienating parent's brainwashing. The distancing parent's brainwashing might be intentional or unintentional.

Gardner believed that parents (mainly women) fabricated false child abuse and sexual assault claims against the other parent to avoid future interaction. Most PAS instances do not have charges of sexual abuse in them.

A cluster of eight symptoms arises in children with PAS, says Gardner. Some examples include a campaign of deprecation and hatred against the targeted parent; weak or absurd explanations for this deprecation and loathing; lack of ambivalence about the targeted parent; strong assertions that the decision to reject them is theirs alone (the "independent-thinker phenomenon"); reflexive support for the favored parent in conflict; lack of guilt over the treatment the alienated parent; and use of borrowed scenarios. Unfortunately, even though these criteria are frequently mentioned in scientific literature, experts in the area have not examined their significance.

PAS was categorized into mild, moderate, and severe levels by Gardner and others. They are expected to rise in quantity and severity as one progresses through the various levels. There is a wide range of treatment options available depending on the child's symptoms. According to Gardner, any change in custody should be based on the alienating parent's symptom level rather than the child's.

Gardner proposed that primary custody should remain with the programming parent wherever possible. Additionally, treatment of the child was suggested to stop the alienation and repair the broken relationship with the targeted parent. In the extreme circumstances, Gardner advocated that the kid be transferred from the alienating parent's household into a transition home before going into the targeted parent's home.

Parental Alienation Syndrome manifests itself in eight distinct ways.

A campaign of slander

Anti-targeted-parent animosity consumes youngsters who have been subjected to parental alienation. After being adored and respected by their child for so long, targeted parents can suddenly find themselves the object of hatred.

Absurd and incoherent reasoning

The grounds given by alienated children for their antipathy toward the targeted parent are not of the magnitude that generally leads a youngster to reject a parent when questioned by a psychologist. For example, it is common for these youngsters to express disapproval of their parent's eating habits, cooking methods, or looks. They may also accuse others of making false claims that they know to be incorrect.

A lack of ambivalence about the parent who is alienating

Alienated youngsters have an immediate, reflexive, ideological support for the alienating parent. This parent is viewed as flawless, whereas the other is considered to be a complete failure. When an alienated child is asked to identify one unfavorable quality of the alienating parent, they are likely to draw a blank.

The phenomenon of "independent thinkers"

Even if the alienating parent appears to have an undue effect on the children, they will steadfastly argue that the decision to reject the targeted parent is the child's own. The child also denies that the alienating parent impacts their attitudes toward the target parent and frequently utilize the idea of free will to describe their decision to do so.

Lack of guilt over the treatment of the target parent

It is common for alienated children to look cold and calculating toward their abuser, and they appear to have no guilt or regret for their actions. As a result, there is little appreciation for the targeted parent's gifts, favors, or support.

Unwavering support for the alienating parent

Whether a family is intact or newly split or long divorced, there will always be disagreements and conflicts. Regardless of how stupid or unfounded the alienating parent's stance may be, the alienated kid will always side with that parent. When it comes to interparental disputes, there is no willingness or effort to be unbiased. Children with parental alienation syndrome have little interest in hearing the target parent's perspective.

Parroting statements from the alienating parent

Alienated children frequently use statements and concepts taken from the alienating parent to accuse the target parent of wrongdoing. These include using terms or concepts that the youngster does not appear to grasp, speaking in a programmed or robotic manner, and making allegations that cannot be backed with evidence.

Rebuffing extended family members

The hatred of the targeted parent extends to his or her family members. The targeted parent's extended family is also denigrated, reviled, and shunned. Aunts, uncles, and cousins once adored by the children are now relegated to the sidelines.

Targeted parents graded these eight behavioral manifestations in a way that was compatible with Gardner's hypothesis (Baker & Darnall, 2007). Parents reported the eight behaviors with a high degree of regularity. Alienated children were able to preserve relationships with some members of the targeted parent's extended family in circumstances when the relative was aligned with the alienating parent, which is an exception.

A study on the adult children affected by parental alienation

Psychologists have been concerned about PAS for some time. Still, there has not been a lot of study on the specific problem of children rejecting one parent because the other is having an overt or covert impact on their beliefs. Research on parental alienation and parental alienation syndrome is lacking, although demand for information is high. Several websites attract thousands of visitors each year. Books and chat groups dedicated to parents who feel the other parent is turning their kid against them are bestsellers, and there is a growing body of research on this topic in divorce literature. If you are a parent

In a 2007 study on PAS, in-depth, semi-structured telephone interviews were held with 40 people. In addition, an investigation of the material was completed. The following are a few of the most important ideas and results:

Differing family situations

Fathers, mothers, non-custodial and custodial parents can all play a role in developing parental alienation syndrome. A post-divorce custody dispute is the most common example of a spiteful ex-wife manipulating the children against their father.

However, that is not the only way to look at it. Many other alternative familial contexts exist within which parental alienation syndrome might occur.

Assaults on the body and mind

People interviewed about their experiences with an alienating parent reported that that parent had mistreated them in one way or another. Children, in their naivete, are apt to align themselves with the parent most capable of meeting their needs, according to these findings. For the most part, the individuals surveyed supported the parent they had grown to depend on and feared losing, rather than the parent who was most sensitive or capable.

Psychiatric disorders in parents

Additionally, it was shown that many of the distancing parents had narcissistic and/or borderline or antisocial personality disorder and were regular drinkers. This additional abuse and trauma variables in the client's early history should be considered when a social worker provides individual treatment to a client who may have been alienated from one parent by the other.

Cult parallels

Cults can serve as a valuable framework for analyzing parental alienation. Many of the emotional manipulation and thought reform techniques used by cult leaders are also employed by parents alienating their co-parent. People who have suffered parental alienation syndrome and their therapists can benefit from this comparison. It explains how they came to support a parent who was ultimately abusive and harmful.

Similarly, a cult member's exit strategy has an impact on the healing process. People can leave cults independently, be expelled from a cult, or get counseling to leave cults. It is more common for people who quit the cult on their own to depart than for those whom the cult has rejected for failing to satisfy its rules and regulations to walk away or be counseled out (Langone, 1994).

Leaving the cult is merely the beginning of the healing process, regardless of how the group is abandoned. When the negative messages from the cult have been integrated into the psyche, it takes a long time and much hard work to get them out of the system. Adult offspring of parental alienation syndrome may have the same problem.

Diverse routes to enlightenment

There seems to be a wide range of methods by which a parent might influence a child to reject the other parent. Interviewees cited eleven triggers in their responses. This is both a good and negative development. As a beneficial thing, there are various methods to transition from being alienated to being aware. Sadly, there is no magic wand or silver bullet that can kick-start this transformation process. It was just a question of time and life experience that prompted some individuals to participate. For some, the alienating parent turned on them, while for others, becoming the object of parental alienation from their own children was the trigger for this.

Often, people experience something like a gradual dismantling of their long-held beliefs, a gradual awakening to a more real version of themselves. Self-respect and a connection to reality were seen as positive outcomes for most participants in the experiment. Although this fact was difficult to accept, they also understood that it had been a long time in the making. They had to face some painful truths, including that the alienating parent did not care about them, that they had probably behaved badly toward someone who did not deserve such treatment, and that they had missed out on a relationship with someone who could have been of real benefit to them.

Negative long-term effects

Parental alienation syndrome (PAS) often has harmful long-term effects. Depression, alcoholism, divorce, and the loss of contact with children later in life were common themes among those who were interviewed. Thus, parental alienation syndrome was passed on from one generation to the next.

PAS tactics

Children with parental alienation syndrome indicated a variety of techniques for sabotaging the relationship with their parents, including frequent criticism of the target parent, constant interference with visitation or communication, and emotional manipulation to favor one parent over another. In a follow-up study of over 100 parents, the same measures were effective (Baker & Darnall, 2006). At least 11 methods were mentioned by at least 20% of the sample for more than 1,300 individual behaviors. Adult children's descriptions of their parents' techniques were similar.

Assisting targeted families

Parental alienation victims require assistance, education, and advice. A social worker's primary responsibility is to educate the client about parental alienation and parental alienation syndrome (the behavioral signs of an alienated child) so they can evaluate if this is the problem.

The targeted parent needs to be taught a series of reactions to parental alienation that can keep the them from being unduly passive or reactive in the face of parental alienation. Parental alienation is a traumatic experience for many parents, and they require constant affirmation and support.

Social workers and alienated children

To avoid allying with the kid against the targeted parent, social workers who deal with children now estranged must be self-aware and thoughtful. They must help children avoid being intimidated or exploited by the parent who is alienating them. Third, to assist the youngster in resisting the urge to select a side, he or she should be encouraged to develop critical thinking abilities. Finally, validation of the child's relationship with the targeted parent is necessary. Social workers may serve as positive role models by valuing the parents they are working with and showing them that they are not worthless or unworthy of respect.

What can you do if you are accused of parental alienation?

If you are accused of parental alienation, your first step should be to ask your co-parent to detail what actions they have witnessed that make them think you are alienating them. Next, reflect on your activities and ask yourself if they may be right. Then, do what you can to portray your co-parent in a favorable light. For example, put up pictures of the other parent in the child's room, tell the youngster how much you admire them, and express your admiration for them.

What should you do if the other parent is making you feel like you are not wanted?

First, consider getting the youngster into counseling as soon as possible and recording all you can. Second, consider filing a motion to alter visitation and custody rights if you believe the alienating parent is having a significant impact on your children's lives.

What can you do to fight parental alienation?

Working to establish a loving relationship with your child is the best way to stop parental alienation. Talk to the other parent about what you have seen in your child. You may want to consider taking parenting classes, seeing a therapist, or even going to court if the estrangement persists.

Do you have any concrete evidence of parental alienation?

Begin documenting any changes in the child's conduct as soon as possible, even if it is tough to establish in court. People who know the child well, such as teachers and coaches, should be consulted to see whether they have seen any changes in the child's behavior. An expert witness is sometimes needed to establish estrangement.

CHAPTER 15: CHALLENGES FACED BY CHILDREN GROWING UP WITH A NARCISSISTIC PARENT

It takes a lot of effort to raise a child. Even more scary is the prospect of co-parenting. In addition, it might be very hard to co-parent with a narcissist. So take a deep breath and calm down a little. Setting limits and getting help can help make the process of dealing with this person easier, even if your ties to them through your children feel interminable.

Even on its own, co-parenting presents a unique set of challenges that can only be handled via a spirit of cooperation. For example, even the most amicable parents may find it challenging to agree on details like child custody timesharing or family vacations.

It is much better for everyone, especially the kids, if you can work together. Narcissists, however, may not be cooperative at all.

As we have learned, there are several characteristics of persons who have narcissistic personality disorder:

- An exaggerated feeling of importance

- A desire for constant attention

- A basic deficit/lack of empathy for the people around them

It is impossible to have a healthy family if you have any of these characteristics.

Ex-partners may even try to use your children against you, according to Melanie Tonia Evans, the author of *You Can Thrive After Narcissistic Abuse*. In addition, co-parenting with a narcissist can provide a lot of other difficulties, such as not being able to agree on custody and other issues. You may also find your ex-partner not putting up a good front for the benefit of your child, or making your child's life difficult by disrupting his or her schedule, appointments, and possessions.

The narcissist's craving for power is apparent in all of these difficulties. This can be difficult to cope with, but unless abuse or other severe reasons exist to keep your ex from your child, it is often a good idea to ensure both parents are in the child's life.

The question is, how can this state of affairs be made to work in the end? When it comes to co-parenting, you may reclaim some of your power in a variety of ways.

Establish a legally binding parenting agreement.

Having a formal parenting plan or custody agreement in place will ensure that all details are documented. To ensure that your ex is not manipulating your relationship, it is best to have an independent person oversee the agreement. Items like medical bills, daily life, and holiday visitation schedules can all be included in a plan. The terms of your custody agreement should be spelled out in full so that there are no ambiguities that the other party might exploit. However, keep in mind that establishing a legal strategy for the remainder of your co-parenting years is an expensive endeavor.

Use the court's services to your advantage.

A court-appointed (neutral) guardian for the "best interest of a child" is a beneficial thing to have.

As the guardian learns more about your kid and their condition, they will make recommendations to the court based on what they know about their situation. Regarding co-parenting, this may cover issues like how much time your child will spend with each parent and whether or not they should have joint custody. Similarly, mediators act as an intermediary between parents to facilitate conversation and settlement. Some jurisdictions compel their participation in custody battles, while others do not. If you and your ex go to court for whatever reason, they may assist you in resolving the issue. They do not offer commands or give any counsel. Instead, parents collaborate with mediators to come up with a parenting plan. An appeal to a judge is then made for this plan to be implemented.

Maintain clear boundaries.

The best approach to keep your ex from getting you riled up is to establish a set of rules for yourself.

Perhaps, for example, you would like to interact only by text message or email so you have time to think through your replies.

Whatever boundaries you choose to set, be steadfast in your convictions. Setting boundaries with a narcissist may be difficult at first, but you will come to realize that they are vital and incredibly beneficial.

Treat your children with sensitivity.

Co-parenting can be a tumultuous experience, but remember to keep your child in mind at all times. To be a great parent, you must put yourself in the shoes of your child and respond to circumstances in a way that prioritizes their feelings.

Helping them identify their own emotions—whether they are sad, frustrated, or angry—is another way to support your child. Having a greater understanding of their feelings can help them better communicate and work through difficult moments. Keep in mind that your child's narcissistic parent may not be modeling or comprehending this sort of good behavior, so it is doubly crucial for you to do your best.

Do not insult the other parent in front of your children.

Avoid fighting with your ex in front of your children, and share specific concerns about him or her with a trusted friend, family member, or therapist. When you insult or fight with them in front of your children, you are just putting them in the middle of something they do not want to be a part of. In addition, it increases the level of tension in the relationship and the pressure to take a stand.

Avoid arguments that are based on personal feelings.

Try to keep your emotions and feelings out of the equation. Anxious or depressed, your ex is likely to enjoy seeing you that way. Treat your communication with your ex like a job. While you do not have to agree on everything, you do need to work together. With this attitude, you may get through difficult debates and limit disagreements to an acceptable level.

Expect adversity.

Modifying the way you think about things may also assist. You may be less surprised or worried if troubles develop if you go into parenting situations expecting some backlash. Or you may be pleasantly pleased if something goes well. Co-parenting can be difficult, no matter how cooperative you and your partner are. Coping with narcissism can make it especially challenging.

Everything should be logged for future reference.

Make a list of each and every thing you need to remember, for example, your ex's reluctance to allow agreed-upon visiting times or any abuse/neglect that is taking place. If anything feels right or is not being carried out as per your agreement, document it.

When it comes to things like late or skipped pick-ups and drop-offs, it may be best to bring in a neutral person (a neighbor, for example) to be a witness to the situation. Custody proceedings will benefit from all the evidence you collect. The tiniest of details are not insignificant.

Consult with a counselor.

Call for help if it is getting too much for you to handle on your own. A certified therapist may assist you in working through difficult situations and finding answers. Reassessing your circumstance might be as simple as talking about your sentiments with someone not directly involved. Therapy for your youngster is not a terrible idea either. Divorce affects your child in a way that is distinct from your own. Children of divorcees may be able to join support groups at their school or in their neighborhood. Ask your physician/doctor for a referral to a child or teen therapist if you observe that your child behaves unusually disruptively.

Maintain a sense of perspective in the midst of disagreements.

Even in the darkest of situations, it is important to recognize what you are facing. Narcissists are highly self-conscious and have poor self-esteem, even if they appear confident on the surface. Rather than being centered on the issues at hand, your disagreements often stem from deep-seated egocentricity.

Having an understanding of this is a significant part of the struggle. The essential thing is that you and your child remain calm and secure at all times. Keep your child's best interests in mind and advocate for them at all times.

Consider parallel parenting

Consider parallel parenting if everything else fails. It is different from co-parenting. This kind of agreement permits you to avoid any contact with your ex at all. Using parallel parenting in highly toxic conditions allows each parent to raise the child as they see fit

.

School concerts, sporting events, and parent-teacher conferences are not attended by parents together. Visitation pick-up and drop-offs occur in a neutral place. You only communicate when there is an urgent need for it. While this may seem traumatic for the child, it removes the possibility of conflict between the parents, which is a win-win situation.

It is also possible that, with enough time apart, you and your ex will be able to develop a healthier relationship.

When and how to proceed

Take action immediately if your ex has become emotionally or physically abusive. Attempt to remove your children from their care as much as possible. Do not be scared to ask for help, even if you do not know where to begin (counselors, lawyers, family, friends, etc.). Get your youngster to a secure location as quickly as possible. This may necessitate a court order. This is where the documentation and record-keeping come into play, of course. Your case will be stronger if you can show that you were physically or emotionally abused or neglected. If you find yourself in a dangerous/life-threatening situation and need to get out of there quickly, dial 911 or your local emergency services.

There are times when parenting with a narcissist feels like the most difficult thing in the world. Make alterations to your approach so that you can better manage what you can. Refuse to give in to your ex's constant attempts to inflame your sensitivity. Do not be frightened to ask for help from your family and friends, as well as from the courts and your local community. Remember, maintaining open communication with your child is the most important thing you can do.

PART 4 - PATH OF HEALING

CHAPTER 16: HEALING EMOTIONAL SCARS

Is there a way to cure emotional scars? Unfortunately, emotional wounds can remain for a long time. If we do not address them, they can get worse, and impact us in all kinds of surprising and unconscious ways. We have a limited supply of intellectual and emotional resources, and emotional distress of any kind consumes significant amounts of those resources, leaving less available for us to use in other areas.

In a recent study, people who are not lonely were asked to imagine being lonely in five years' time and then given an IQ test. They saw massive drops in IQ just from a thought experiment about imagining being lonely. This illustrates that when we are in emotional distress, it affects our ability to think properly. Loneliness and the human heart and brain have a close relationship. A press release from the American Psychological Association stated that loneliness was a greater public health risk than smoking and obesity combined, and that loneliness can raise the chance of early death by 14 to 25 percent. Unfortunately, we rarely see the true impact that loneliness and other emotional wounds can have on us.

Anxiety and depression are two of the many effects of loneliness. For those suffering from loneliness, it is important to remember that they are not alone. There are people around them who can help, it is just a matter of seeking them out. Conversely, just being around other people does not necessarily mean you will not experience loneliness. Lonely individuals are often married or in relationships or families. They will often engage in small take, such as whether or not they have milk, of if their spouse has paid the electricity bill or not? But there is no actual connection. Similarly, you may have many friends on social media, but very few genuine exchanges in which you meaningfully engage with another person. Social media may also make us feel lonely or melancholy, as several studies have shown, but the effects are more complex and depend on how we use it. Loneliness can drive us to be risk-averse when it comes to reaching out to others, so instead of engaging in conversation, we are more likely to scroll through our social media feeds. This self-perpetuates since we are more likely to feel alone and depressed.

Loneliness can be a problem, but it also comes with a nasty hook: It generates two perceptual errors, which can be danger-ous. People around us appear to care less about us than they really do because of our perceptions. The second issue is that we devalue relationships unwittingly, as if that person was not worth that much to begin with, and we tell ourselves that seeing them would not be all that great.

So, what can be done to interrupt the cycle of isolation? A leap of faith is required to take action and establish contact, even if you believe the other person is not interested. To avoid challenging situations, avoid reaching out in a way that is either self-deprecating or confrontational. Assume there is a good reason you have not been able to get a response from someone in a month. Emojis are a good solution since they are non-confrontational, but they are also effective in getting the tone of your message across. Because unclear statements like, "I have not seen you in a month," can be a touch unpleasant, added a smiling face can soften the blow and avoid any misinterpretations.

When you are with those you care about, have conversations and ask questions about how they envision the future or what they reminisce about from the past to start deepening those relationships. Curiosity can go a long way, and it is fascinating to think that the cure for loneliness might be taking an interest in someone else, making sure they feel seen and heard, and making sure that we feel seen and heard as well.

As children, we learn via repetition, failure, and trial and error; however, as adults, when we fail at important things, such as a promotion or a job interview, we might be more emotionally invested in our failures. Failure tells you you are incompetent, and that is what people who fail at many diets will tell you. However, it is not about the diet but rather about their system. And most people's default system is to beat themselves up when they fail. At a high level, we are saying that there is hope.

However, it is important to recognize that if people are suffering from emotional wounds, they do not have to be a victim. They can step up, learn to heal and change their life, but it does require effort, and perhaps even some self-compassion. It also requires an understanding of why you may have acted a certain way in the past. Self-assessment leads to personal development and self-improvement.

To deal with emotional wounds, you have to be emotionally uncomfortable. But I believe that even if someone is currently going through a difficult time, there are ways that they can endure it. Go for a nice walk and do some self-care, and allow yourself to fall in love with the person you are becoming – that person who, in spite of having gone through so much, is still standing. Acknowledging yourself for taking actions, and for seeking out something you desire and something you deserve.

CHAPTER 17: TAKE CARE OF YOUR NEEDS

For effective narcissistic abuse recovery, you must begin to give yourself unconditional love, support, and attention. You may feel as though prioritizing your own needs is selfish or morally questionable. You may even be unsure of what self-love is

Many times during your narcissistic relationship, I am sure your needs were ignored or brushed aside as if they did not matter. In addition, the constant derailment of your life by the narcissist and his or her continuous projection of his or her behavior onto you (making it all out to be your fault) would have completely shattered your self-esteem. After a traumatic occurrence such as this, it may feel like ascending Mount Everest is simpler than showering oneself with unconditional love and encouragement.

After all, you may have been doing the opposite for so long. The narcissist has always been more interested in you than you have been yourself, which is evident in your interaction with him or her. And a common reaction to being blamed and tormented by the narcissist is to become critical of oneself.

Before starting to make an effort to give yourself the love and encouragement you need to heal, I want you to know that this hardship is typical.

Changing your behavior might be difficult at first because it feels so foreign, but once you do it, you will see that it has the power to transform your life in ways you never expected.

I want to show you how to start giving yourself true love and support in order to move ahead in your recovery. Acceptance and personal accountability are the keys to moving ahead after a traumatic experience.

Non-healing and true healing are two of the opposites I see in my work with people whom narcissists have abused. Non-healing occurs when an individual's ability to thrive, let alone recover, is severely limited. True healing happens when an individual's ability to succeed and recover is greatly enhanced.

What makes the difference is whether you want to grow through the experience or get through it.

When we use our narcissistic experience as a springboard to heal and improve our lives, we progress.

Narcissism can only be dealt with by shifting our attention away from the narcissist and onto ourselves so that we can heal our pain and anxieties. If we want to remain in agony, it is not easy to accomplish this. To get healthier, we need to commit to mending ourselves. When we remain angry, we maintain a severance from our true selves.

Transitioning from Angry to Acceptance

The emotional agony becomes intolerable as soon as we start criticizing ourselves about how horribly our life has turned out. We have thoughts such as:

- How did I manage to remain for so long?

- How could I have fallen for this?

- I am a complete and utter fool!

- (However many) years of my life have been squandered.

- My life has deteriorated to a level of horror that I could never have imagined.

By blaming someone or something other than ourselves (typically the narcissist), we attempt to alleviate the emotional distress while simultaneously increasing our sense of helplessness.

To recover, we must first understand why and how we may accept what occurred without judgment.

Our unhealed portions necessitate that we face, love, and assist them in a nonjudgmental way. Self-acceptance is the key to unconditionally loving and accepting others.

In the end, it is all about you. It is up to you to take good care of yourself, love yourself, and help yourself grow. It is all there for the taking.

This makes sense to me now. It was essential to my rehabilitation, and it has been for many others. Taking responsibility is the first step toward healing. Certainly, the person is an unlovable narcissist with whom it is impossible to have a healthy relationship. But it is important to focus on healing the unhealed parts of yourself that made you so vulnerable to narcissistic abuse. You will have a healing journey that goes far beyond anything you had ever imagined.

Before meeting the narcissist, were you 'full and happy?' Many people who have been abused by a narcissist are incredibly capable and independent, but they are not emotionally full people. After a long period of being single, it is not uncommon for people to encounter narcissists. However, the question of "Was I whole?" and "Did I have ideas about myself and life that allowed me to be whole?" resurfaces.

There is a big difference between accepting that you have un-healed portions and accepting and healing them, and taking on the guilt and blame.

When we cannot accept this, we feel shame and guilt. Changing our emphasis from guilt and blame to the pro-active energy of creating what we want – rather than being stuck in what we do not wish to – changes everything.

It is time to ask yourself the two most important questions.

"Why would I continue to hold onto resentment when it is just going to bring me further emotional agony?" And , "Why did a narcissist fall in love with and remain in a relationship with me?"

When we are ready to face these issues head-on and take respon-sibility for our own well-being, we are in a position to begin the process of healing. To start dealing with these questions, you must overcome your ego and open your mind to new possibili-ties. Your ego craves justice, retaliation, and accountability – ego has to be "right" and "wrong" simultaneously. To attain "justice" (which is impossible if you are attempting to do so out of a place of misery), you would only feel better for a short period, and then you would feel much worse. When we use our egos, we can produce nothing that lasts long term, feels good, or is sustainable.

Let your ego go at it for as long as you like; the result will be the same – you will continue to hit brick walls and feel pain until you finally accept that true healing is all about dissolving your ego, realizing it is your internal enemy, and that the ego's blame and shame are all products that take you away from your liberation and not toward it.

Self-Responsibility

What is the point of self-responsibility? If we do not have it, we believe everyone else is to blame, and we do not modify our behavior. Taking responsibility for your actions does not necessarily mean accepting blame but rather making a choice to heal and develop and become better as a consequence.

Acknowledge and accept that there are portions of yourself which contributed to your vulnerability and powerlessness as a victim of narcissistic abuse. Accepting this allows you to focus on repairing the areas of yourself that are still unhealed. To make lasting changes in your life, you need to accomplish this.

How to Recognize Your Unhealed Components

Before beginning rehabilitation, you must recognize that suffering, guilt, and humiliation are not in any way connected to becoming better. Recognize the parts of your body that were abused. Before you were in a narcissistic relationship, you may have had these characteristics:

- I was never complete or content with myself

- I needed some accomplishment or someone else's approval to feel good about myself

- I had unresolved issues with previous relationships and had not accepted or healed the unhealed parts of myself that surfaced during these traumatic relationships.

- I never learned how to love and accept myself "simply for being myself completely."

- Obsessive and compulsive thoughts about "what I should be doing" kept me from just "being" and enjoying my life. I thought I was only lovable because of what I could do.

- Often, I was my own harshest critic instead of talking gently, supportively, or even accepting praise. I could not let others into my life without feeling they had ulterior motives or were trying to manipulate me.

- There were times when I questioned my ability to honor myself and set limits rather than relying on someone else to "love" or "honor" me.

On and on and on and on and on...

Your connection with another fake person directly results from your failure to be true to yourself (unconditional love and support).

If you have learned about narcissism and identified the narcissist in your life, it is time to stop blaming others and take accountability for your actions.

To begin the healing process, victims of emotional abuse should have **little or no contact** with their abusers. Nonetheless, victims of psychological abuse may still deal with the aftereffects of their trauma, such as recurring flashbacks, nightmares, anxiety, dissociation, sadness, and poor self-worth. In addition, due to the strong emotional attachments formed due to the abuse, they may feel compelled to check in on or re-connect with their perpetrator.

Continuous self-care techniques as an adjunct to treatment are effective strategies to begin caring for one's mind, body, and spirit after abuse, together with help from a trauma-informed counselor. Experimenting with therapeutic modalities and discovering the ones that work best for you may be highly effective. Consider adopting the following practices:

1. A state of meditative awareness

Executive functioning, learning, memory, planning, emotion management, and attention are all affected when traumatized.

Some of the parts of the brain that are affected by trauma, such as the prefrontal cortex, the amygdala, and the hippocampus, can be improved by meditation (Lazar, 2005; Creswell, 2015; Schulte, 2015). Meditation has a favorable effect on the brain's neuronal connections, causes an increase in grey matter thickness in parts of the brain associated with emotional regulation, and a reduction in our natural fight-or-flight response. However, having no contact with your abuser might be more difficult when you are meditating since it helps you become more in sync with your emotions in general. Taking a step back allows you to examine other options before acting on your impulses, which might impede your healing process.

2. Yoga

It stands reason that a practice that incorporates both mindfulness and physical activity might aid in the healing process after a stressful event has occurred. There is research to support the benefits of yoga in relieving depression and anxiety. It has also been shown to enhance self-image, emotional regulation, resilience, and self-esteem in populations at risk and symptoms of post-traumatic stress disorder (PTSD) following domestic violence.

Dr. Bessel Van der Kolk, a yoga researcher, says that yoga's self-mastery helps traumatized people reclaim control of their bodies. Trauma survivors can regain a sense of security in their bodies. When we re-connect with our bodily experiences and engage in forceful movement, we can begin to release the trauma that is held in the body.

He says, "I would say the bulk of the folks we treat at the trauma center and in my clinic have broken off ties with their bodies. Their body may not be able to tell them what is going on. Somehow, they are not aware of what is going on around them. This led us to realize the need to assist individuals to feel comfortable with the feelings they encounter in their bodies. ... The benefits of yoga for those who have been traumatized have been well documented. ... An activity that requires you to pay close attention to your body, especially your breathing, can help restore the brain's vital functions that are disrupted by stress."

3. Anchoring to the truth.

In the aftermath of a breakup, survivors are particularly vulnerable to abusers who try to revert to their lovely, deceptive personas to get them back. As a result, you must not only ban your abuser's phone calls and messages but also eliminate any social media connections you have with them and their supporters. After a breakup, you will have a fresh start to reflect on what occurred and how you felt, rather than being influenced by the abuser's attempts to paint a different picture of events.

If you feel yourself being drawn back to an abusive partner, start by writing down at least 10 instances of feeling humiliated by your connection with the narcissistic abuser. This will help you begin the process of anchoring yourself to the truth. Refer to this list whenever you feel the need to contact them.

To address any potential triggers that may surface while anchoring yourself to the reality of the abuse, you should engage with a trauma-informed counselor. It might be difficult to shift your attention away from the positive parts of your relationship with your abuser, but doing so can assist in alleviating cognitive dissonance. Reducing this dissonance is essential to your commitment to a successful recovery.

4. Self-compassion and inner child work.

Your association with your abuser may have brought to the surface additional traumas that you had previously suppressed. In times of emotional distress, it may be necessary for you to comfort your inner child as well. As a result of this incident, your childhood needs may have been exacerbated, necessitating self-compassion.

Those who have been abused are often plagued by poisonous guilt and self-blame. Despite their rational understanding that the abuse was not their fault, it can nonetheless reopen old wounds that have never completely healed. This might be a symptom of a greater problem of never being satisfied with one's level of success. Healing requires a shift in negative self-talk since it challenges previous narratives that the current experience re-inforced.

To comfort yourself when these deep-seated feelings arise, imagine you are speaking to a person you truly care about. Write down some positive affirmations you can say whenever you are grieving, such as, "I am valuable and worthy of true love and respect," or "I have a right to all of my feelings. I am entitled to a peaceful existence." As a result of this self-compassion, it will be easier to continue No Contact.

Keep in mind that when you are self-blaming or condemning yourself, you are more likely to participate in self-sabotage. Conversely, your self-worth is reaffirmed every time you accept and exhibit compassion for yourself.

5. Work out.

After being abused, a daily fitness routine can save your life.

When it comes to working out, choose a routine that you love and stick with it. Begin small if you lack motivation. For instance, instead of committing to an hour of walking each day, set a goal of 30 minutes. As a result of exercise, we may replace the biological dependency we build with our abusers (Harvard Health, 2013). Our abusers' highs and lows reinforce our attachment with them by releasing hormones like dopamine, cortisol, adrenaline, and serotonin (Carnell, 2012). A healthy diet and regular exercise can also help alleviate the physical impacts of misuse, such as weight gain, premature aging, sleep issues and sickness.

After a period of emotional abuse, you might look forward to a new and more fulfilling life. Of course, you can live and thrive, but only if you are willing to put in the time and effort to take care of yourself.

CHAPTER 18: DEVELOPING A STRONGER CONNECTION WITH ONESELF

There are two types of people: those who enjoy being single and those who do not. If you fall into the second category, single life can be painful, especially if it seems like everyone in your life is in a relationship. However, if you allow it to be, being single can be a blessing in disguise.

Being in a healthy relationship has its merits, but we seldom consider all the benefits of being solitary. According to psychoanalysis Babita Spinelli, L.P. and psychotherapist Megan Bruneau, M.A, the following are only a few advantages of being single:

Developing a stronger connection with oneself.

As Bruneau points out, when we are in a committed relationship, our partner constantly reminds us of our values. While it may sound like a cliche, being alone allows us to concentrate on our relationship with ourselves. "We can learn to go inside for encouragement and support...[focusing] on our connection to ourselves and converting our critical inner voice to a more compassionate one."

Having a clear-cut idea of what you want in life.

It is possible to discover more about yourself while you are alone, Spinelli says. "There is a greater sense of self-awareness and a willingness to spend time with yourself." When you are constantly changing partners, you tend to lose sight of what you want and who you are. When you are single, you have plenty of time and space to figure out what you want in life.

Holding yourself accountable

It is up to you to claim yourself responsible once you have figured out what you want and how to spend your life. Spinelli explains that you learn to carve your path and develop inner confidence and resilience while you are single. "You are authorized to make your own decisions and hold yourself accountable for those choices," she adds.

Non-romantic relationships are nurtured and deepened.

Strong friendships are just as crucial as sexual connections, if not more so. They may improve our lives in the same and even greater ways as romantic ones. According to Bruneau, we have more time to focus on ourselves and other vital connections when we are single.

Time to relax and recharge.

If you have always liked the idea of starting a side business or taking up a new pastime, you will have more time to do so than if you were juggling your time with a significant other. When you are in a relationship, it is not uncommon to feel like you have less time to do what you enjoy, says Bruneau.

All the decisions are yours.

When you are single, you do not have to compromise like you do when in a relationship. "Do you want to take a few weeks off from work and travel around the world? There is nothing to worry about," Bruneau adds. "Do you want to relocate to a different city? Go and do it. Decided not to spend the holidays with any relatives? It is all yours!"

It serves as a stimulant for development.

Finally, being single may be a powerful force for personal progress. As Spinelli explains, "Because they are not negotiating between their own wants and those of their partner, being single frequently inspires a person to turn within and better care of themselves psychologically and physically.

What if you are surrounded by people who are already in committed relationships?

Being single can be particularly difficult if your single friends are disappearing like flies and more and more couples arrive in your sphere of influence. As Bruneau points out, there is a lot of guilt and worry associated with "failure" to find a romantic companion. We tend to internalize being single as an indication that we are unattractive or unlovable. But, of course, this is not accurate.

According to Spinelli, being unmarried and even "unsuccessfully" dating might elicit feelings akin to grief. But remember that no two people's paths are comparable. Having friends in committed relationships forces you to address this uneasiness and come to terms with it as you discover how to be content as an individual without a significant other. And, as Bruneau points out, making new single pals is never a bad idea.

How to be satisfied as a single person

When it comes to finding happiness and contentment as a single person, here are some ideas:

Prioritize your other relationships.

Bruneau thinks being single requires you to be more proactive in making connections with the people in your life, but it is well worth it. "Isolation/disconnection almost certainly leads to anxiety and sadness," she says.

Make time for self-reflection and self-improvement.

During this period, you get to date yourself, be your lover, and treat yourself with love and care. Take a break from your day-to-day routine, like treating yourself to a lavish dinner and bouquet. Spinelli advises, "Take the time to figure out what you desire in life." In other words, it is an excellent chance to go on a "date" with yourself and discover who you are.

Expand your horizon

Consider joining clubs, taking lessons, or starting a side business to expand your horizons. Bruneau advises, "Take advantage of not having to work around someone else's schedule and having free nights and weekends." If it is something you are passionate about, you may devote your time and energy to whatever you want. Spinelli says, "It is an opportunity to pursue new interests and activities that bring you delight.

Make new acquaintances and spend time with those that are single.

Bruneau says establishing new friends can help you build a stronger network of individuals who understand where you are coming from. Having pals who know what you are going through, she adds, "Is incredibly vital."

Make sure to take care of your well-being.

"You can focus on your self-care without concern for balancing it with your relationship while you are single," says Spinelli. Regardless of how you choose to take care of yourself, make it a priority.

Discover who you are.

Bruneau recommends "practicing self-inquiry and self-compassion." When you put in the effort to get to know yourself, you can clearly define your goals in life and understand what you want from yourself. Then, if you would like to understand how you might be preventing yourself from achieving the life you desire and deserve, you can consider working with a therapist or a life coach," she advises.

Do not hold back.

As a single person, you have much freedom. When it comes to events and vacations, "enjoy being more spontaneous," Spinelli advises. "You have complete freedom to go where you want and do what you want. When you are unmarried, you have a lot of flexibility to construct the life you want to lead."

Set objectives for yourself and focus on your development.

When we are single, we have the opportunity to take responsibility for our actions, support ourselves financially, and set our own goals and objectives. Use this time to clarify your goals, whether they be personal, financial, or otherwise. Take a moment to appreciate how far you have come whenever you achieve a new milestone. Spinelli says, "There is a power that is created when one is alone."

Maintain a clear head.

This might be a fantastic time in your life, and you do not want to waste it by being down on yourself, says Bruneau.

We all deserve self-love, regardless of whether we are single or in a relationship. To reap the benefits of being single, you must enjoy the time you have to yourself and utilize it wisely in order to develop your feeling of self-worth, sense of value, and clarity on what you want. Even if you are in a relationship, there is nothing better than going on a date with yourself, enjoying your own company, and appreciating yourself.

CHAPTER 19:
START LOVING AGAIN

After a breakup, whether right away or decades later, we have the most incredible opportunity to heal from the inside out so that we will never have to encounter the same struggles again. But we cannot accomplish this by trying to replace a love partner with a new one, as someone would do if their dog were run over and they bought a new puppy to replace it. This will just bring us more of the same!

After a near-death encounter, it might take a long time for us to feel ready for another relationship. For many of us, the most important relationship we need to build is an unconditionally loving one with ourselves.

When you do this, you will come to see that you are the person you have been missing in your life all along, and it was the absence of self-loved that had forced you to give your power to abusers in an attempt to earn their love. But when you learn to love yourself, you will realize that you will never have a better friendship than you do with yourself. This means seeing ourselves as a source sees us: lovable and worthy of love and the good things that life has to offer, just as we are. It also means understanding that if we can let go of the internal and external trauma that hinders us from being who we truly are, we will be able to live an extraordinary life and find true love. True love has to begin with you. Remember that isolation and loneliness are two different things. To put it another way, aloneness allows us to use our healing hiatus to transform our life and love potential beyond previous painful patterns.

'Love Beliefs': How did we acquire them?

Love is the source of all greatness, and when we love, our connection to life, ourselves, and others is heightened in wonderful and amazing ways. Our hearts can be sparked by a beautiful flower, or by a child's grin, or by caressing our pets, or by a loving hug from someone we care about. But many of us believe that avoiding love is the only way to prevent the catastrophic conviction that love hurts and even that love might demolish us.

So, how did these dreadful love myths arise? They have to do with our former lives, epigenetics, and repeated adult love traumas, as well as our painful childhood experiences. We have had terrible encounters with people who have busted our hearts open.

For many of us, this occurred as a youngsters when they were completely reliant on caretakers who may or may not have been healthy and caring. Our energy fields were already pre-programmed to carry the traumas of these painful experiences before we were born (science is now proving the truth of epigenetically inherited trauma). The patterns continue through childhood and into adulthood until we can change the trauma pattern deep within ourselves.

We can release these traumas and liberate ourselves from the fear of love so that we may show up in love healthily and securely while simultaneously being kind, strong, and self-honoring.

We make new decisions when we change our beliefs about love

As long as we have done the inner work and learned how to navigate love healthily and safely, I can guarantee that we will be able to connect with true love that is truly rewarding. False, unhealthy, and dangerous love begins with a bang and quickly degenerates. It takes time and patience to find your true partner. Respect and consideration are the guiding principles behind it. A sense of camaraderie and a common set of ideals are the foundations of this kind of relationship. It extends and increases with time. Throughout a relationship, a person's feelings for the other person grow deeper and more meaningful. And this is fascinating because our relationships may reflect our healing relationships with ourselves.

A deeper and deeper relationship with oneself develops over time while on an inner healing journey as we shed trauma and bring in the presence of the Divine within ourselves.

Those who truly care for their innermost selves treat it with the utmost respect, care, and wisdom.

When it comes to love, we no longer live in a world where "instant romance" is synonymous with "fairy-tale-love" or "if love hurts, it must be true." It is time to let go of these falsehoods, which we know will bring disappointment, heartfelt anguish, and even abuse.

We must also cease thinking that love "simply happens." It is not the case. Love entails being crystal clear about what we stand for, whom we can have a meaningful connection with and then acting as per those ideals.

Being in a healthy and gradual relationship with someone is a sign of true love; it involves taking the time to learn about the other person and determining whether or not they are the right match for us.

We have to treat ourselves with the love and respect that allow others to realize our value and how to treat us if we have come from prior relationships where we gave power away and clung to abusers.

Real love is not always easy. Being a decent person is not only about going the extra mile for the sake of doing nice deeds for others. But, even when your beliefs are not matched, you can love someone enough to let them go and no longer hold them responsible for not providing you with what you had hoped they would.

True love also entails taking on the gift of your development to keep creating your truth with yourself.

The myth of happily ever after

True love involves letting go of the expectation that all relationships must end happily ever after, and that they are a failure if they do not meet that standard. When we terminate a relationship because we are afraid of what will happen if they break up with us first, or we cannot bear the notion of being in a relationship with anybody else, we are bound to suffer. Even though we were unpleasant and hopelessly unsuited to them, we may nevertheless be afraid of this.

You might also be afraid of terminating a relationship or ashamed of ending one once you have made a connection with someone, so you find any excuse to "go along" with them even if you know it is wrong. But, unfortunately, that does not serve them or us in any way that is kind or honest.

Love, power, and safety

Now that I have recovered from narcissistic abuse and re-established my relationship with myself, I realize that my capacity to show up honestly in relationships is what keeps me safe. I am honest with myself about what kind of relationship I am for, in order to connect with a new partner on a soul level.

With you approach relationships from this angle, narcissists will reveal themselves to you. If you give them some time and do not make excuses for their behavior, they will demonstrate their lack of morals, empathy, and regard for others. Likewise, people who lack the resources to be a loving companion will have a superficial connection with someone who does not fulfill their needs, and they will have a difficult time attempting to make them do as their narcissistic tendencies dictate.

Are you ready to be and connect to true love?

Are you ready to expect the best in love, and to offer your best in return?

The only way to overcome the scars we have been left with is to be willing to put in the work necessary to repair our emotional scars on our own terms and for our own cause.

Thanks to my healing that has taken place, I am now confident that love is for me, and I want to experience it first and foremost as a healthy, kind, and powerful outflow to others.

CONCLUSION

A lot of what goes on in a relationship, breakup, and subsequent attempts at co-parenting make sense once people learn what it means to be a narcissist. But, unfortunately, narcissists are not often labeled until after a relationship has ended.

Self-importance, an insatiable want for attention and praise, strained relationships, and a lack of empathy are all symptoms of this mental disorder and describe narcissistic people. It is crucial to learn how to deal with a narcissistic co-parent, and how to deal with this type of behavior in general.

How to tell If your co-parent Is a narcissist

What are the telltale signs of a narcissist? Empathy, disregard for others' emotional well-being, and need for approval and attention from others are among the most common characteristics. However, how does this play out in a partnership of co-parenting? The following are some telltale signs of a narcissistic co-parent.

They blame you for everything.

Narcissists frequently believe they can do no wrong and that everything is the fault of those around them. One of the most recurrent signs of this in co-parenting circumstances is related to scheduling concerns. They may strive to make things difficult for you to see your child. Or they may interfere in your child's plans, causing them to blame you.

They fabricate.

Narcissists are notoriously dishonest and care little for the consequences of their actions. For example, they could promise the kids a large birthday celebration but then disappear on a solo vacation, all while saying they are en route to pick up the kids.

They appear to take pleasure in the conflict.

It does not matter how strong a couple's relationship is; conflict will inevitably arise in co-parenting. However, narcissists like the attention and emphasis that comes from creating conflict when none exists. For instance, you have agreed to alternate custody on Saturdays. "I do not know why you do not want me to see the kids," a narcissistic parent may remark to generate drama.

Children are used as a weapon against you.

Narcissistic parents frequently use their children as a weapon against their spouse or partner. To penalize the healthy parent for creating boundaries, they may threaten or use the children to convey messages that should be communicated only between parents. They may also persist in communicating through the children even after being instructed not to.

Texts from narcissistic people are a common example of how they might chastise and criticize you daily for your parenting skills or lack thereof. Make the conscious decision to stop replying to or even reading these texts.

The use of disparaging language about the healthy parent to the children is another prevalent approach in this situation. For example, children of narcissistic parents may be told that the other parent is not a good parent, lies, uses drugs, or any different number of lies to make the children doubt the other parent's integrity.

Parenting in a parallel world

To successfully co-parent, both parents must be mature enough to put their children's needs and interests ahead of their own and maintain a respectful, cooperative relationship. Unfortunately, when it comes to narcissists, this is rarely the case.

So, what can you do to better the situation as a parent when dealing with a narcissistic individual? When it comes to raising children, parallel parenting is one of the most effective methods. To put it simply, it is assuming that what occurs at their place is their business, and what happens at yours is yours. To make parallel parenting work, here are a few recommendations:

Gray rock

Gray rock may seem strange if you have never heard of it. However, it is based on the assumption that narcissists require emotional fuel from the other parent. Narcissists can go out of their way to make you feel hurt, angry, or resentful. Imagine a gray rock in your garden. All of the same hues, there is nothing special about this. When dealing with narcissists, you aim to become as expressionless and immovable as a gray rock.

You may think that this is straightforward, but it is not as simple as it initially appears, since a narcissist's primary purpose is to make you angry, and they are typically excellent at it. Furthermore, because this individual has had a close connection with you for a long time, they know precisely what they are doing when getting that reaction from you.

You can become like a gray rock by focusing on being as objective as possible and answering with facts. Try to avoid disputes and react only to inquiries that are directly related to the children. Avoid talking to them whenever possible.

Set yourself up for the least possible contact.

There is some coordination even in parallel parenting, but the more you avoid the narcissist, the better off you and your child will be in the end. Co-parenting apps can be quite helpful in this situation. Using these apps, you can keep track of significant dates, sports schedules, reimbursement requests, and even scheduling conflicts without ever having to speak directly to the other parent again.

Your child's Social Security number and health insurance information will already be in the other parent's database, so they do not need to ask you for it. "It is in the information bank on the app" is a very gray rock response if the other parent inquires about this information.

Even in the most extreme instances, you may have to confine your communication to the app and not via phone calls, text messages, or emails. In high-conflict cases, some family court judges have mandated this form of in-app communication. There is an instant and easily available record of when messages were sent, viewed, and what they included.

Do not involve your children in the conflict.

Not only is it necessary to not inform your children that the other parent is narcissistic, it is also important not to speak adversely about them. Although it is good to explain the situation calmly and objectively, it is also important to avoid eliciting an emotional response.

Many of the narcissist's manipulative methods, such as gaslighting, speaking poorly about the healthy parent, pitting siblings against each other, or using the kids as pawns to get to the other parent, may be quickly figured out by youngsters. Let your kids know that they can trust you to be there for them whenever they need you and show them that you are a healthy role model.

Self-care

The greatest self-care advice I can give you is to seek out a coach, counselor, or other professionals who have dealt with narcissistic abuse in the past. Your self-worth and the validity of the strange things that happened in your relationship are essential to your well-being.

The following are a few recommendations to keep in mind:

- Let your body speak to you. It is tiring to be in the company of a narcissist. It is as though you are riding a never-ending whirlwind. Allow yourself to rest, sleep, relax, and simply be.

- NO CONTACT. Keep your distance. Do not engage in any form of internet stalking or harassment of any kind. If you need to speak to them, do so through someone else or compose a letter to express yourself. You open the door for them to walk straight back into your life the moment you reach out.

- Surround yourself with people who are good for you. After a breakup or divorce, it is typical to feel the need to separate/isolate yourself. But when you go out and socialize, you will feel more like your old self.

- Do not be afraid to express all your emotions. Do not bury your feelings. They are there for a reason. So let them out. Let your feelings out by slamming plates, crying, or talking to yourself. Let yourself feel the emotions you are experiencing. You will feel happier and more liberated the more you let them out.

I hope this helps. All the best!